£3·99

/48

DREW MILNE was born in F
Scotland. He lives and works in
Olsen, and two children. In 199
the Tate Gallery, London. His b
(1994), *Bench Marks* (1998), *Th*
(2001), and *Go Figure* (2003), ar .... Kinsella, *Reactor Red Shoes* (2013). He edited *Marxist Literary Theory* (1996), with Terry Eagleton, and *Modern Critical Thought* (2003). Since 1997 he's been the Judith E. Wilson Lecturer in Drama & Poetry at the University of Cambridge.

for Dell, Frank & Astrid

DREW MILNE

IN DARKEST CAPITAL

Collected Poems

CARCANET

First published in Great Britain in 2017 by
CARCANET PRESS LTD
Alliance House, 30 Cross Street,
Manchester M2 7AQ
www.carcanet.co.uk

A CIP catalogue record for this book is available
from the British Library, ISBN 9781784104900

Book design: Luke Allan. Typeset by Richard Skelton. Printed & bound
in England by SRP Ltd. The publisher acknowledges financial
assistance from Arts Council England.

CONTENTS

IN DARKEST CAPITAL collects a number of previously uncollected, unpublished or privately circulated poems, along with the following books and chapbooks:

Satyrs and Mephitic Angels (Cambridge: Equipage, 1993)
Sheet Mettle (London: Alfred David Editions, 1994)
How Peace Came (Cambridge: Equipage, 1994)
Carte Blanche (Kenilworth: Prest Roots Press, 1995)
Songbook (Kirkcaldy: Akros, 1996)
Bench Marks (London: Alfred David Editions, 1998)
As It Were (Cambridge: Equipage, 1998)
familiars (Cambridge: Equipage, 1999)
Pianola, with Jo Milne (Cambridge: REM Press, 2000)
The Gates of Gaza (Cambridge: Equipage, 2000)
Mars Disarmed (Great Barrington, M.A.: The Figures, 2001)
The Damage: new and selected poems (Cambridge: Salt, 2001)
Go Figure (Cambridge: Salt, 2003)
the view from Royston cave (Cambridge, 2011)
equipollence (The Song Cave, 2012)
Burnt Laconics Bloom (Old Hunstanton: Oystercatcher Press, 2013)

Poems from 'Blueprints & Ziggurats' and 'Lichens for Marxists' first appeared in the following journals and publication contexts: *Jubilat, PN Review, Blackbox Manifold, Cambridge Literary Review, Poetry Wales, This Corner, Island, Public Pages, Crrritic!* eds. John Schad and Oliver Tearle, *Yellow Field, Openned Anthology, Lana Turner, Infinite Editions, Journal of Linguistics, litter, Plume Anthology 3, Plume, Poetry London, Wolf, Zarf, datableed, Chicago Review,* and *Painted, Spoken.*

IN DARKEST CAPITAL

SATYRS AND MEPHITIC ANGELS

'… paradise was never attractive; it was accepted as part of the bargain because it meant the avoidance of its opposite. This did not yet make the negation of the negation, or the negative dialectic, into a product of secularization. But it suggests the invaluable historical advantage of being able to say that the Messiah has not yet come. What has already been can only be disappointing. The chiliastic enthusiasts of both sacred and worldly peripeties have always understood that.'

Hans Blumenberg, *The Legitimacy of the Modern Age*

SATYRS AND MEPHITIC ANGELS

Go litel bok, invoice these strain line shadow inks,
or suffer in silence imago mephitis,
I can smell your poison squirt of ingrained chalice,

squids in blood-dust of leavening slates, it blakes too,
or as art suffering dusts this its antique time
and that there monstrous word glory in suffering.

A dangerous demagogic word holds us surely,
like the masses the measure *is* suffer; for these
abolitionist crudités, as raw mangetout,

may smash up (*piano*) while your smudge spill barks out
beyond purely verstehenden explication,
in these hand sewn diagnostics of future past.

If as tool performed the so forth poises genie,
angle as massage stones of which the knights Templar
will build over geo-roof folie de patrie,

and not notorious dress codes of tea-room zones,
in memoriam tears torn in atomiser
stutter sprays: but which public takes this reading room

challenge to continuous administrative
contacts? We press on in class marks etching wretches,
we as two roles flush out imagoless twinnies,

touchstones plate these nail grimy as naught or nothing
under the optic sun: d'you know it too, lumpen
prole boho, all declassé like fat sump fury,

eh fairy with the awful smell glues mephitic.

DOLPHIN SONG

Would I were as Arion, or as the story told,
choosing harp fish swordpens to take the plank, the egg,
the swallowing passion in supperless *díke*.

Where is that dolphin now? we still adhere to the
doctrine of redemption which originally
connoted a slave purchasing his liberty:

not to change its world but to escape this, it has
flown off the wheel, off grief's thole misery while vine
sprays against are its expenses. For dolphin song

no season supposes such slavery orphic,
while urban revolution remains roused as lyres
for the hungry he hath filled with such good things, of

which one among is hunger *anánke*, potlach
expenses defrayed deformist, details lacking
as if normal proceeding will follow slaughter,

or our harmony parts dissolve clear and brittle.

A DREAM OF PELAGIUS

That trump of revelatory will-lessness breath
avers how pre-Arctic the *lapsus* never was,
never Adam's before graceless worldly games pall

and all to the din of make it thine, wanderlust
times where no tour like it he dreams, as rushes breathe
and the snow-bunting pains, nesting monkish homes

(pre-gardens), before the yes worldly cross-treck terns
all dovecotes mysterious return, while saying
like ptarmigans want the *genius malignus*:

I am not nor hope be lest this history yet,
but as no locust trip fastens down epistles,
nor if we define progress as burning gold eagles,

will oblige this dissolution in camel shirt
reaching, past oblivion straws, and, ascetic,
wait skua's revenge on burning magnesium.

Gulls disgorging throats cry *food, where are my lies now?*
and gash to treachery, as will you read me in
fragments, so press on dark glacial char, these glooms

heirs to progress, where dreamer declines flock waywards.

THE IDEA OF ORDER
AT HABERMAS-PLATZ

What about then as if Cant of Latter Day Saints
is adrift, white feathers, malgré tout adrift seas
singing bugger thy hymns alas amid ilex.

These no-churches in pages dust community
are blest satellite and video monasteries;
I kid you not word-smog petroglyph-boulevards,

just sing anthems to the tannoy blue mountain blend –
thy lord think on of hard times revolutionists
that is this my yellow and coffee dust halo.

Stop for orangeade in class struggle museums
where druids of domestic diamat dial
adjust down our Lady of the Garden Centre;

so alphabet *ratio* in D.I.Y. Church
dawns on fishers of networks puritanical,
all undistorted or wish-sweet as bliss revenge;

sound bite angel, go wholly public spherical.

ENTELECHY: MARGINALIA

A dispiriting melancholia screen burns,
regardless with crouch brow diffusion, reams against
sorrowful natural history, its weight of

facies hippocratica now to well up
with proper dues where landscaping peters out in
forlorn, petrified thimbles and plastic tears.

There's roads across to fashion hermitage where all
out with the must pass muster, curdling instruments
of resumption, as erring no blood letting fails

the succour memorial of blood, in them there hills
where wordless deforestation, without reply,
is the back catalogue of ironed out anger.

This rush drowns out familiar species lament
in the accurate strain upon half-line gardens,
as fresh caught ruins of herd doubts and tired love sigh

in the book of wells lascivious, *if it's fine!*
and aimless eclipsing furrows the banished plod
of its sincerely crisp phenomenology.

Lichen sidles against their arid kenosis
and will be jargoned to those *guitarra* yes strains
by those back to second nature word boys of *ach!*

expletive decay, rewarding for *plein air* stills,
just yearning for that anorganic sybilline
rivalry of being in print, hark hectoring,

like as could the species pass away better yet.

DENIZENS OF LOW STREET

All along the low street hopes akimbo, and plants
wilder but denizened out spit it, upon this
cobble sliding hurts all midlothian drag-heart,

while the mile's bilious rain *smiles better*, which now
castles into palaces we have not outlived,
and feels blood apocryphal drive the denizens,

vomiters, and *ye of scant hope* shuffling among
rucksack rashes, to wish some purdah for to be
and not notes on the decline of Scottish murder.

The Sappho parchment clasps our bitten horizon:
there is pornocracy, which no pibroch here sings,
just as still water runs deep swimmingly below:

pray tell, not calmly, to lease punctured yearning clans,
is it this way lies mercat ahoy festival;
go and Campbell it out along the soup high way

autobahn to Glencoe, while you stake the low roads,
I'll die before you, fit-you-saying speak-easy in
pop furious ballad style: *Warhol? I'll Warhol you!*

That lettre à d'Alembert misweighed how the
civic joy can be stationed for the tart riposte:
under three crosses mercat you can spot the ball,

here of all places, and you thrill to hideous
cork thrust damage remissness of *where I belong*,
as those in dicky birds drooping groove their night-piss.

That vamp still acts, dreaming eats of tourists for tea,
whose ghost con-tours will not bring back the silver birch,
and the cambered *pace* macadam rolls sighways,

while beneath, children pass for the well clad courtless,
playing private nursery courts in romper suits,
states streamed as united colours of brash refuge,

but *will the car be ready*, dreams wild one freezing,
still refusing the grim one bar heating cross road,
as residual rockbearing slough subsiding cries:

Nova oh no Scotia, lime my sheepless north face.

DAYMARES

It was easier to keep on than wait for days
to shorter get, allowing night speak day-mares their
turn to rust amicably amid thoughts silting hope;

no imagined that could not falter, needing nights
back to imagine with when the city silts too,
searching for what unseemly newness, unsilted still,

to save a heat where satire crumbles, or a past
catching on to this new temerity, its weight
of action as rusts no longer amicable.

There is no bleak suffice, no text unbound to bleakness,
as would be, when all around lose theirs. *Come clearer!*
no suffice could unyet or relinquish injury,

want, so many little deaths, boring the shiners
upon quick graves of angers, or is it lonely
passing among without heed for exile therein.

Don't suppose, would it, that by-the-by clocks off, while
awash in daymares and nighting lamps of waste our
goods selling bads the very dregs knew odious:

discussion is waged on alarmist, in alerts,
by sofa or by crook, or *sang froid* pachyderms,
but raptured hurtwise tracks regret *to hope dusting!*

as in truth to say mourn for the past circumvents.

HIBERNATIONS

The shadows are longer, out of touch with its times,
but the geese-steps of accommodation bristle
and are still life no more, you know the *kind of* thing;

O money, O function, O job, lend me just the
private and confidential, dazzled convictions
of the prevailing *absolutely wrong,* or so.

It's all over bar the accountancy and the
dispiriting fibre of the nevertheless
necessary reticence. Old hat, can I not

eat the psalms, the blushes, the feigned departures,
and then the kandym, perchance to skip from tuber
to tumour, abashed at the violence of critique

in toyish, dyspeptic, slow-grilled embarrassment.

THROUGH THE BUY-OUT JARGON

I am virus soul corp, hug me to this unreal
viral city which had not thought, death undone, so
short term many fun-funding were this captive class;

for our soul libidinal pulsations referred,
hush fund breezes cyclone my well-products esquire,
or are greenfield ventures as this stock cubism falls.

I am aid pack, cash-crop and pearl mint tax heaven
with airs, seedcorns, graces skeltering pro or fits,
yours contumely, or old use-value as am used;

but cashing chips one in, figaro appliqué,
these now machine tools bitter this dream crop decor,
appellation cash vortex, wonders contrôlée,

as atrium hollows words which do not pass go.

POSITIVE INDISCRIMINATIONS

The male my hermit and manner view, or it ill
be easier to amble you, as sod the count's
odd sadeian bosom: that twizzle of velour

authenticity ligs on diners card before
currying distemper: *thus fresco!* as it grew
too astart its vile pink and mildew narcissus.

Your after personal lather shaves conditions to
the grain, and sandal would glows penumbra, like raised
faculties lathed to *is it me you're looking for?*

I'll be buggered doubt if it ill be easier
to trekky from cling-on to boldly woe, wrecky
from hornblower, as my toy captain flies undone

to the oh so moby dick. Stand out in flux, my
chassis, *go getty get two!* where a rival peers
so in dissidence are personality glues.

Can it for cried out loud be ill, this bolster blust,
where muzzles so militant are discriminate
particular wars losing dots to incisions?

Woe aquamarine boy ogles a-gloop, fish tank
a-breathing, *might as well* plunder your theme tune's youth,
breeding goggles as Irish masques unflint the stones

which are teething *the Troubles* in this Trumpet town,
as glorious good would await the orange monsoon
marching season: *will it be veiled rivers of blood,*

or the world well lost, washing soldiers dreams to the
foot of iambs? How now, brown cow, sacred brownie
of a cubbish clout, will it come in bull-dog chants?

My wall to wall crumbles, fondling what its falling
reason suffices, and I'll Hemingway in slow
motion, if you'll be mine buster, this double oh

sever me shaken and lotus-bond stirred: it's me,
yes flirty, *oi polloi*, and I'll fame you baby,
like no transcendental *epoche* ever could.

Camera my maybe as I fleet it to crashing
guitars! and sheer out to one big man walk for one
kind man, in head-brides revisited while gloaming

cities groom unquiet, but as mental suers
gutter-press it, I am as ill as resources:
does it feel good renouncing discrimination?

I bet! *Well I'll be*, belower me willingly,
I canute not these kingly waves, but despair the
eponymous women and children from sieges,

while old uncurl dunder-bluss is the unveiled pause
of all kiss, whose lips chrome the enemy salvoes
training in play boy plasticine pavlov artwork.

Still it looks like trouble, *it looks like there'll be more*,
but candle my armour random bores, I'm just an
amicable man, who spays distance aargh moor dusts

of uppishness and beaches lust spermaceti
for *hope the mastodon*, spolia opima
of reason's amble to homo erectus, as

veiled shaft members ingrate diction shamble it so.
Passed out to out pretty, *I know you* the *son*, my
fathead farmer will be as worn by the hand-downs,

aging deceased repent! But as no demiurge
I'll libertine time in gnostic bliss, or is it
blisters, it harm you will harmly done, yes blisters,

calmant to the sleepless still caffeine trot, and thus
zealot erectus, homing my consensus, if
not saving face secrets himself is man, or would

as awe man for awe that *me you're looking for* is.

IN MEMORIAM JOSEPH BEUYS

I

In gripe lore rumbles war among moderns
      the humble it dreams wet
these hold all penchants for how to pay
      lisp your r around Rimbaud and go all
impresario mon juste
      for thieving abates
but not the look as contemporary mingles it
howl mid-atlantic coyote
      fat sucker lush
likes Beuys like Beuys likes publicity so
      this even if Andy troubles
what with what politics *what's yours?*
as fifth international slow gloats demise
consolidates inc
      among diverse others
slow boating it to audience participation
      behind you! in chat show chews
we're warming up for pause core grain-
less sepia relents in cut up
      burrows *all together now!*
sweating last human pieces my contact
      there faded
sepia genitals in tattoo smile from old calendar
      relents still to *in the know*
shining in my irony plated social kills
nice to see you yes it's delicious
wishing seconds like no felt tomorrow
      slow down the pratfalls
harmony guise shines freeze innuendo and
hurrah for applause man standards we can
      on cue *like it!* Dalai Lama cosmetic

as answer drifted back over remote mine-
lands of a dead star not very
call me cute
call me what the hell you laugh for canned.

2

It's all hands on ship my feckless sea persons
drop curtains we'll futurist in rich disturbance
ahoy art-less! viral shows shout against those
we're Just-In-Time that's JIT! for go-slow
                    All out! our future ist franchised
                        down sound bites ye petty *bouge pas!*
            pun along a few don'ts on Sunday we bleed
or shallow it through to mid price laments
                    toads of woad hole you bore us
we'll go all eco art trash cosy if you don't
        sit up and pay cable
        subscribe there *follow the leader!*
we'll be no ad man's throb flush prize job
twitching to first over the wall corp ego
                    our sounds bite back fat sucker
        jealous Maecenas from slash cut prices
the Texas in memoriam trophy shudders
to the standard oils of Folger juniors
get out of conglomerates get into Shakespeare
                    ye olde facsimile hoards *it pays!*
                    a word from our sponsoring angels
award your bliss markets and *get compact!*
or is that weariness rather than perspectival
spread-sheet autocue *ho, ho! on camera one*
        you mean we never meant
        it that play so fast we must
        scratch ahead the wireless
accustomed to the sped words *buy now!*

no dirge but in mono-breath jive talk junk
        you groove we track
        encomiums and viral breath
        blows its own sales to sirens
this is your life the bellows wheeze where none
        coyote howls to straw ideology without ideas
cloudy in places where these scattered showers
purpling in damask sash that nought a muses.

3

Jelly roll fat pack culture strolls complete
on I don't know but yep it's all here in grey
for a live one saddest of all moving pictures
        just listen and underwear charming
pants off I'll flag mine to *see the tie slip!*
dialogue yep surety sure
           wait your snatch through meals
for more hot dinners than we have feed back
        it's in the pink
    but even comes a turn to eat mics
you'll speak like journal pit bull scholion
avante! avante! the changing of the guard
        me fat sucker – you coyote *dig it!*
all substrates to the impresario gel
        neo-neon *check that, alright!*
teeth to the chisel eyes right
        storm troop to pithy apocalypse
quick march as masochism ghosts mountain
        wherever whenever we gather
there's always one cries *yeah!* among us
    cut up amid prelates howl on those
unspeakably long lines no agenbite sounds
    done the work *get it?* know stuff
as corpses oeuvre it to blessed philologist

in double-breasted Achilles-mouth harm-
ony for its next trick *please, you're too kind*
        while indianola instrumental novelty
      fox trots to *Every Kiss is the Same*
           how's that coyote?
speak up cry wolf no metaphor murder but
roll on worldly lit. bugs jiggering *no really!*
gathered here amid self-publicity
        hymn me
      our text is *Tonite!*
      your host is shame
and the art of psalmody de profundis I belch.

NO FLIGHT OF EONS

Wingless angels ashen to turn sybaritic,
these ark tones harm its pedestal marmoreal;
then blush our chiliasts, this adamic profanes

whereas pebbles disinter, crumbling unwraps rheums,
still is as stones of dead matters chimerical,
whose diorthosis pores over veins willing spores:

these cherubic ruins through all wish go jussive.

READY-MADES IN VOGUE:

a student's guide to capitalist poetry

✄

IN A STATION OF THE TUBE

Fashion intelligence:
do trousers work in the office?

VISION OF THE MISTRESSES OF ALBION

Ceramide Eyes Time Complex Capsules
are small enough to fit in today's tiny totes.

THE RAPE OF THE LOCK

Poochie salons are hot news
with the shampoo and jet set.
It's debatable whether people
and their pets look alike, but
there are definite similarities
in beauty regimes.

SARTOR RESARTUS

The clarity of shape, proportion
and colour is the absolute joy
of the international collections now.
All confusion and contradiction is
past. Such moments of single-
mindedness in fashion are rare.
This reductionism – paring down
everything to that which is wearable
and flattering – can work for everyone;
not that everyone will end up looking
the same. Failing all else, pay attention
to what you do with your mouth: outline
it with pencil, apply a colour that lasts
all day, put your lips together and blow.

TINTERN ABBEY REVISITED

Introducing lip spa, its patent-
pending formula delivers water,
nature's own best moisturiser,
liposomes, vitamin E and
soothing botanicals in 31
fabulous shades. Indulge.

THE ETERNAL RECURRENCE

Colour is back – in clothes,
in films (Almodóvar, Tim
Burton, cartoon-mania),
in art (Pop revisited),
and, it seems, in restaurants.

THE LOVE SONG OF W. H. SMITH

Scarcely a page of this lusty
blockbuster goes by without
some reference to the leading
players' state of tumescence.

HOMAGE TO MARINETTI

Dune driving is so much fun,
there must be something very
wrong with it. In an inversion
of prudent daily motoring, speed
in the face of the unknowable is all.

THE HERMENEUTIC CIRCLE

Whatever the problem
we've developed the answer.
The result is a range that takes
caring for your hair seriously –
because we know you do.

MERRY WIVES OF WINDSOR

There are still sparklers
on the ground floor, of course,
and special customers can
talk over diamonds and a
sweetmeat in a private
drawing-room at the back.
It takes about two minutes
at a too-rich-to-run stroll…

ON RE-READING ADORNO

This time it's not kiss curls
but frou-frou from a
soap-opera graduate:
the curled lip, the flick
of the fringe, and the
hard-core sashays mean
serious rock business.

THAT NATURE IS A HERACLITEAN FIRE
AND OF THE COMFORT OF THE RESURRECTION

High Definition.
Lipstick that speaks
louder than words.

For a perfect behind
spend twenty minutes
on your bottom.

THE ODYSSEY

In an age that is aware
of the fragility of the globe,
people are asking more questions
before they set off on holiday.
The travel publishing industry
reflects this, and has been
developing a conscience
for some time now.

LEGENDS OF THE HOLY GRAIL

Names that once existed
only in geography lessons
and Trivial Pursuit –
Anapuran, Aconcagua,

Everest, Patagonia, Zanskar –
could start appearing
in your photo album.

THE NATURAL HISTORY OF THE C.C.C.P.

From left: pilot's eye view
of the approaching volcanic
summit of Mt. Vilyucha;
lunch on trek, including
limitless quantities of fresh
salmon caviar; wild irises
in the gentle valley of
the Zhilovaya river.

THE ANATOMY OF MELANCHOLY

Our comprehensive range of corrective
procedures for women and men includes
body, breast, face, nose and ear-reshaping,
eyelid surgery, Collagen replacement
therapy, varicose and thread vein removal,
permanent eyelash line enhancement,
baldness reversal and a unique non-
surgical treatment for the ageing face.

A HIGH-TONED OLD PHENOMENOLOGIST

A new vital force,
Rénergie, acts on the
cellular fibres which
determine the quality
of the epidermis.
Result: a double
offensive against the
signs of time passing.

A CRITIQUE OF DIALECTICAL REASON

Between Sea and Sky
a new wave of makeup.
The colours run pale-to-torrid.
The collection introduces eye-
coloring: a new liquid-to-
powder formula with a
difference – it glides on
and stays in place for hours.

TARMACADAM SCABS

for those who have died on the roads

*'He who approaches metaphysical problems without proper preparation is
like a person who journeys towards a certain place, and on the road falls
into a deep pit, out of which he cannot rise, and he must perish there; if he
had not gone forth, but had remained at home, it would have been better
for him.'*   MOSES MAIMONIDES, *The Guide for the Perplexed*

LULLAY

Water churns,
radiating the distance;
alive in a vicarious future
into uncouth world icommen ertou,
which gets on
            with humming along backgrounds
to atmosphere hiss of sulphureous skies,
as rubber
            rumbling of carburettors
abbreviates
            the night illumination.
There is no easy stumble to dismay,
lollay, lollay, to car ertou bemette;
all must falter,
        glad-handed into praise,
                into the ruins of realism
where, amid a stray
            rust screech of axle,
we seems an orchard refrain,
                            combusting
    with don'ts,

and, hatched back to carbon static,
don't is all the charge attrition distilled.

QUITE CONTRARY

Swete lemmon,
      wormes woweth under cloud
as hallowed spoons
     cuddle
          these silver racks,
so soft cherry fair
       is out of kilter;
but brush low,
   the tackle is
    sweeping still,
where the call
      goes to die before sleeping;
but each gome glit forth as a guest only
in angry mists
     of loaming
     care-weeds
cherish the dull
   as how our garden grows
new skin eruptions,
   groans,
       will wart wrinkles,
ears all cauliflower to Castaly,
while swete
    lashes of I,
   resting,
        as if
there is more rancour in the dust flying.

GUTTER-SNIPES

Thou teres werne,
      woshe away the blody tern;
it is grooved peace,
 in space
            between pages,
this lost pace of bindings,
    now gallows-birds,
as cardboard
     cities paint skinned blisters
              still,
furiosite and wodness of minde,
where gutter blood pitches
   mucous affray,
then street arab
        or nomad gutter childe
pipe wynsum snippettes,
        or word-fire crying,
who gains precarious
   livings, trifles
streetwise,
 or as shallow troughs pasted on
     narrow
     posted curbstones,
     water-coursing,
sing of a maiden that is makeles.

TURN AGAIN

CAR-SHAM-YE or give way,
> will you ever

subside,
> as eaves into coal harmony

follow seeping strips
> of fool's dust gold-ramps,

chipped into road-bones
> paved with tomb-ground stones,

muttering DAUNGER,
> steel-rattle, accidents

at work!
> widening boulevards against

cobbles
> that melt into milk-bottles thrown,

into air-less gnathic parking refrains,
and into cat-flattening hits of
> *excuse me,*

I am Alpha and Omega,
> road-maps

for waters in the midst of the street of it,
paved with pure,
> as it were,
> transparent glass,

and whosoever was not sparrow-foot splayed
in that book of life,
> knew no firmament

only drip-dry
> shirts
> of leaflet concrete.

GLOSS

Cats-eyes clouding over
       turning   gloss tears
to shine
     each shifting
          autumnless halo,
mushrooming into the creeping overgrowth
of endless braid,
      as the gilted lapels
hold me
     from the halo headed wardens,
who read the matted floor as woven
                grids,
where small scale
       mosaic
       enclosures
persist in such corrosive atmospheres
that the choking tears
         knows its street bib
is all software,
     shuffling to
     weeping lines,
as the saying goes,
   and texture   refrains.

ACCIDENTS

The snail of slaughter passes
                    through the dream
or order,
        showering its lost tickets
    all the way round
            the skirting cattle traps,
as gig lamps breathe prowlers,
                        the bullet trains,
    the harvest of iron,
        rolled out to chip-sewn
    thinness,
      for dancing bird-men with speech-scrolls
    and lost relatives:
                or at any rate,
    blood-letting deemed acceptable
                        in stone
    caught as petroleum film on lip-stained
    cups,
            where we find evidence of the love
    of polychromatic effects
                    contrived
    by inlaying
      and, conversely, crash scratches
    in reliefs, so called,
                unnaturally   exposed.

TUMULOUS BURIALS

Trailing the hardly,
        its crushed notes crackling
and spattering
  into these har-broken
bits of paint-carving
              byway ornaments,
where weather prevails
  as mother of faces
seen like, *look there!*
        though draining in search of
microliths,
  the dominant form of which
was the crescent, with its black blunted by
bipolar flaking
        giving a marked ridge,
were presumably used to arm weapons,
these men in the moon-dots
            scuffed into lines
among other specular
       residues
of old bone-shaker
   plate-spinning
       remorse.

STILL LIVES

❧

A STILL LIFE IN BLUE

Key in your chosen sore digit light codes,
as asphalt on blue notes, or pin connects
there to ease, is lay numbers, an affray
turning savoury or blanched / as I would
        have it, and am vulgar
        with pensionable posts,
        ground and down a grand
piano we call the last waltz through the
institutions. Still you catch a mid-frieze,
a rift, whim or sundry windlass in awkward
name squads tuned in drops of out, the out-looks
        bleached, come all overcome,
        resting sherry on yawns,
        as per fucking usual,
while famine stalks rash dispensing kindness.
One stone into the beach clears flock circles
where sandboys blether geodesic laughs,
the last on these no-hoping scorn dancers
turning where the rash begins. Where do the
yellow lines start to quiver, break surface
aghast or harshly tendered out, lose brave
and face all arteries, all passion fruit
and all the lust accrued without design.
        If is hardly the party
        to which were invited
        all the old hopes / none.
        Lungs cry slurry, asbestos,
        then mesothelioma

brushes the known roof of this construction
with premature dust related ill-ease,
then unremembered dies. I don't hear it
any more than the sky respects yellow
lines drawn across its long loss of music,
where airs dance into the unconsoled rooms
without which thoughts of those already dead
have no cadence or respite from wishes.

        If you would, it could be
        perhaps this last perhaps,
        sarcasm kissed
        as sarcasm does,
        its minor artforms
        blowing death blushes,
which visible thorns remind us is dark,
as all the seriousness I yearn for tries
to let bliss in on the secret. Once more
the red rust of the night sky seems human,
or humanly lit by spark and light trains
trundling awareness and so much harsh freight
that clotted scars, eyeless, dark flowing blood
may curdle the calm to scorn, as I do.
A chain letter courts your close affluence
in human affairs, asking the diagram
which laughs back, what it is to be hoped for
and can be done, what it is to be loved
where a group breathing calm stills the light fit
embrace of a memory song, a first
flush choir in this possible power.

        Don't will be this slogan,
        curling around the grievous
        bodily harmonies, where
        music is as music does,
where the mean time foresees a lengthy close,
and where red army choristers release
their agent purple loves. As around gills

of salmon drinking tanker blood, a dash
to mediocrity sucks new smoothness
while abhorrence wells in wet gravity:
        this *now* suppurates,
        this negative equity
        of fouling penitence,
        falling grouts with the lies
of fast statues a particular scorn,
for what now will kill these ease chariots
of star-struck news casting seamers, remorse
in absent-minded city, where once but
pity, is blush decadence now gone grime.
        Arise sweet fire of tempers,
        thorns in upper hall
        picture moss, blaze resin
        in scars of tithes dripping still
with meagre truth stipends played hereabouts;
throw frieze knots to cloistered embroidery
of such poached hope, ivory blessed charm-schools.
Chattering class, pine on arrogant pie;
blend on, quaff fluted slave sung righteousness,
        while happier walls
        might fly through breeze,
        these cobbles crush, and trees
        hum bomb ballast drones.
The sun baked velvet of revolution
might coordinate our tepid dissents
in catatonia, as graphs are bliss:
there maps the lost symphonies, tone dismay,
comes on fresh but is all over, happy
as we who sold this free, this crocus called
defame, sold lays to flee obliquity
or mumbling sing of shame. But crash / this quill
conforms to bills in awe commanding flaws,
leech-love until no purpose stills the glow-
worms tricked in gauze who will have brutal force;

trees hum sweet subsidence
rivers chanted for oil wars,
or shoots at the holy fruit
of blood stone planted.
Loose leaf meets blade and gravely weighs flagrant
winter tourists, whose psalms on trade now roast
and fade a rash on dry forests. Still none
be so in harmless no
that dreams a curse refined,
whose glaze grows patina
or dusting slow, varnishes
the blind weasel bluff of street-wise word husks,
a size it little profits to bust. Still/
famine eyes in grainless sighs fall brittle
or nonplussed, while every state meant murmur
creates the wash and blends in airless hate.
This world awaits a glaze of angel pens,
but I renounce weapons of happiness
and the petals of blood which kiss such hope-
less greener grassless: 'Shoot into the foot,
I say, and only then into the air.'

A HOST: ITS SUNG REVOLTS
for Andrew James

These favours of abstraction are spun out
lost hostages whose wafer thin resource
is child upon child, while grey-scale cattle
shadow crust the marvellous plastic sheen
thinking every thing but the prisoner
is a potential weapon,
is a host of lit tissues
charring the hope funnel

47

with cinders and resin and memory.
Down to the last tilt of the wish split head
there is a frenzy which awaits even
> the wary trust of walls,
> as pyramids and frisby
> play love upon love, the song
is brass tap trances to which the fridge hums
it still kills me, wills the drip familiar
to turn uncanny the hush flesh pink gloss.
Our cowering wounds wish for bark lashes
of rubber or cork, but find only glue
tears, its bald glitter gilt by a city corps
> which reveals no bonded scrip
> or water marks, upstream
> of a wind of contagion.
You are a cut above all that. This is
a felt suit in an immaculate glove,
do not try to touch it even with your
slow eye and gloss: we are its matt finish.

A CITYSCAPE: ITS AUDIO AIDS

Patchwork roof patterns float in lung landscape,
weathering well a part scope of empty
in cloud stroll letters as dead as buttons,
stood in unfamiliar aging city
> whose homeless door on freedom
> sings embalmed remembrance, quilting
> lineaments of granite leaf
> and lantern jawed features,
an unlikely posture in groaning rose,
for lip silence over unstated sky –
in a whole flock distant of bizarre rock

and vessel of second breath: some gave all.
        Nor ever lose, what is what is /
        where others give horizon,
        o vanished eyes, we are as far
as the eye could see still on stalks of loss;
divine hiss of nefarious blood script
what imparts name to such silent ague.
Death like a vice came abune them mid bane:
        he rax't out his hand
        on his ain lown frien's,
        lips pairtit sweeter nor butter,
        his heart a raid, finer
        nor oyle an yet nakit,
as hush of wall holds brittle dry relief,
a harp's cry in awkward vigil smiling;
it is a corruption and hoary frost,
a discus wreath in wind-chill facts of home.

A GRAMMAR OF DON'TS

Wormwood slates pry misrelated dressage,
steely as stunned foundry stone vermifuge,
and desk stark maximals radiate 'if',
as digging on the skeleton a church
was found, foundered, for the like unchartered
        is veridical, is trace
        mentals strung in a red grace,
        irons stroked spectacular thin
        or the like used as conjunction
        crushed in some dumb fiery AND
        like you must do like I do,
chiming mottled periotic marrows
with winsome reluctance in predicates

so blank, incomplete, that I never have
and never will believe that. Varnish sticks
in rash bland wishes and fell ornament,
and tells autogravures awry to slump
            mumpish; there is this sanded
            hollering for grand junk spliced
            in sulk teams. This is hard
            and even harder than
            the first lesson. The there seethes
and I do not think much of him batting,
but their risk spiders blend imperial
on diplomat geist-vetted web clover
            in a pink blood wash of breath
            on a map that never dries.
            I cry to think as much name
            flies in flakes or might as well
            willow in this vice versa
            velvet crumble of voice.
These sort of sweets are not good. Then again
as in marks is plain there be no plural
verb strung with neither, nor, each and every:
neither summer nor I were at the school.
These are our floundering flip height crest falls,
            curdling our open meeting
            same sky, now glum plundered
            for snow glint charge, trundled
            through postludes of error,
            our crust done us porcelain
            sung on crass piano, since
one must do as he's told by their teachers.
There, there! still glows patrimony reviled,
coat turned on redundant actually
trailing gift stress tubers whose blow root is
neither misuse of shall and will, but can't,
though I will go in the pictures tonight,
            were it not in rush blinkers

snow-drops and suddenly rooves,
with semen immaculate
lobe spun in plaintive arrears
as young real lung is rationalised, as I
would be glad to hear from you, or shook free.
A clasping hand shines the time it takes to
stammer, for eyes in multitudinous
turn sallow, the flesh distempered solvent
to a new cardophagus,
then mislays its not so perfect
infinitives amid which
I should so much have liked
to have watered down or been. It is not
enough then or style, calming this misuse
of dues sung in price aggregate affects,
when due to an accident he came in
late, for whose soft machines whispering wet
in smart gels and alloys
is cost taken in hand,
a loft projected, from
bruising a preposition
and back. This was different
from what I expected
and worse. Cubes of bone-derived gelatin
colour in pop party lung talc showers
flowering into this misuse of than: no
sooner had he started than the bell rang,
soda streamed from still love in a needless
sentence, ending with a preposition:
what did you do that for?
Literate conflict is love
or a starved declension
parsed in cash crop consensus
and then flung in short ages shared by all,
our other wrong songs and casing pronouns
used as relatives for mortal don't-hopes

in our floundering stand. This is the man
whom as you know gave us the flag, with stripes
and all stabbed through in inconstant cosmos;
                    distress flared from shifting slag
                    all the don't is smelling salt,
                    the one what I was looking for,
                    kissing me luck for true finals
                    where words wrongly understood
                    are right enough to die happy
                    and lie: do not aggravate me.
Do not is the lie of the land, love sunk
in shimmering dialecticisms
whose foodless passion is this: we have been
waiting on you where the misuse is all
our ands willed in dissimilar clauses,
a crude ark of hard-working claims where we
is a one who has prospered in despite,
trembling for that don't start in nothing willed.

A BREATHLESS CAST
a bagatelle for Anton Webern
shot in error by an American soldier

A breathless cast demands early forests
gulping harmony inks in jet kisses
liberating marvellous noises off,
                    or perhaps quiescent
                    revolts still sweetly stir
                    to underline voices
                    wistfully whispering
without xylophonic yielding zephyrs.
A briskly curt don't estranges, feeling
for faces gone, half heard injured jaw keys

listlessly mouthing no, nor never on:
>   overt pizzicato quirks
>   resist such strife torn unction
>   under veins worn with wounds
>   worn with weathering xmas
>   your yodelling zugzwang.
Awkward borders clash driving east, flying
for familiar grace hearts in justice kites
laughing mysteriously nerveless oaths:
>   pleasing poisoned quotes
>   rapidly resolve sorrow,
>   their timid tongues
>   under vivid winter
while we're xeroxing yesterday's Zion.
Agony bathing calm drowns earth forlorn,
grounds grown harsh if in jewel kilned liquids
like level melancholy now owns our
priceless qualities remorselessly swathed
then ushered vacantly worsewards with war
wishing xerotic yawning zestlessness.
Ashen breezes clasp dead ethers for friends,
>   forgetting grim haste
>   in jarring Kriegspiel,
>   leaving loaded mordents
>   nightshades now opulent
over old plangency quite restless sung,
til tides undermining venom's vaults will
wither xenophobia's youthful zeal.
As bagatelles collapse, daft ease finds fear,
>   falling for gauche hope
>   into joy jaded kindling.
>   Lovelessness might mourn
>   mortals newly oblique;
proud pain quilts revolutions so strangely
then tempers us under unarmed visions
while waspish x-rays yellow your zither.

A MODEST PREPOSITION
for the people of East Timor

Gnosis means simply knowledge, of whither
we are hastening, though in other times
it is as if one met song murderers,
death hands whose sacrifice is body fact.
               It is not so difficult
                    to see the advance stand still
                    on circle line excursions,
swan-dancing over the pre-scribed pages
still cultivated as our last chapter,
whose neck turn thought is to be all the same
                    though its pain never is,
                    while the tread 'essential'
                    is nought but read ends,
where that something to be said is here blown
before an altar of bad-mouthing calm
that has every thus crust appearance
of being consecrated now to prose;
                    perhaps a sophist delight
                    first composed dissoi logoi,
                    if fraught, mark the old turn,
with the vengeance of communication
whose firsts are a thousand island dressing
cooked in fine archaic illustration.
The result is a disaster, flesh lows
                    as the spits turn critical,
                    the state of delirium
                    signs its fault, and its purpose,
like so much else politic dullness, is
not to cure one single flesh rash richness,
much less deliver us from the old stall

of some moment dress
whose tardy expatiation
is a fashion of *other*.
In a very framework of city, law,
or our covering stillness, is only
a drift, striving to obscure that poor will
the polis spent its meaning creating,
like whether to wage slaughter
or just send observers:
our own plenty questions
face us like blocked capital,
apologies on part half of people
do not ring true, and besides, nothing here
indicates what is still called election,
as to pass, from divided opinion
to bloody confrontation, is rather
the current of this *stasis*.
In the other form of trance,
on sponsored Dionysus
or the bold insomnia of sold news,
the wine has a happy dish, with brilliant
shivers drunk deep, singing home sweet heimat.
A clumsy proposal, then,
for the swift abolition
of *all* our advertising
from cable to leader and hope,
whose possible first pleasure
may be a beginning
on vultureless beauty
drained of litanies and winged messengers
whose further angels assist the carved drapes
of actually existing capitalism.

Bland I strands unaccomplished into glove,
or what is worse, there hoarse ply is flat hum
sublated soul quite overcome on reefs
collapsed as aster folds in diremption,
til shoals of stunned wonder rock forth and crack
           into dumb ligature
           like this, this or is what's worse
           a shimmered pinching wind
           which blends in natural salute.
There, there! everything is a serration,
a pain whose pages unfold their collapse
in a loose leaf calendar of lost love,
where the less said frays in blank thrill lashes,
and the night shifts a broke still heart, saying:
           I came, I saw, I wept,
           am sunk simple in all
           as is, or there was more,
           as there was there tearing
where no lets suffice flickers a skin tight
in the hunger trumpet mechanical,
folded cool over melting flesh whose stung
can you spare a change, can you? or will you
rakes the hatchet of its sun for buttons
whose loss is this comfort aura ahoy,
this cart in time, which bleeds in already
           breathing strokes of shamble fire,
           through pastel tinted glove,
           where sirens sing revolts
           of love, and its silences.
I have wine and you have your sore junction
clasping ages of steam in tinder bracken
that fears a rustle burn of distinct grief,
or is this embarrassment all the love

the puncture kit provides?
perhaps it be a back place
where the pavement is in parts
for our winter wrists and ration of crisp?
The questioner tires these firmament zones
with a patience we forgive but can't live,
as dust smiles filed all aboard sell so well,
so flowing in palimpsests
while sun chemical dyes
would grace the arch passing
half misgiver about to break into step,
and run towards a slow revolution.
No spontaneously resonant wing
feathers this drift of kissed lung
whose bird song is tombless
in unquoted pantheon
where a fine line refrains,
confirms our kiss frills and still less installs,
while bitten sung, we are in home grown thirst.
Breathing seams the brittle less than sleepful
if which passing becomes our hesitance
or best all wishes reach in porous arts;
hold palmy like the reach, the glance declined,
hold the line this while, a drift or glimpsing,
whose sunken like still bitters
and is not all the same,
is shot round arcadia
our capital nest of sleep
feathered in albatross germ.
The ultra centre beats heart to pumice
til loss flourish is its quick air column,
flagged in ingenious false mosaic
and bird sung drifts fly in hard cries of thirst
in many screaming breezes
amid no special corner
wherever clouds are mournful;

memory quilts cast that ration of nerve
over whose unthinkable none is passed
and lost in an indolence we call love
as though we were fell asleep on a fire.
       All aboard the light same
       liquid in soft reprise
       don't no go a please sweet
       pretty gull disposition.
Capital, it folds us now, go on trees,
a sleeping log lies dead in your nature
shake your money makers in gruff whisper,
       shake your barrage balloons
       your accident of city,
       a midriff in shy petard;
go on, shake, the rage of fashion is age
or at least blonde desuetude, whose twist
in tongues is the colour of your money
as motions engrave scars in untold stones.
       I call out as a candle
       whose glove learns to be brisk
       about this quiet season
of ruthless dismay, but which is all late,
is all the comfort blanket rose, but then,
don't mind me, I'm only minding my hopes.

A STIR WHOSE COLLECTS RAGE

Out a bleach familiar cusped is a loss
bleeding with *cannot*, a thumb dried leather
soon to be glad ragged in lip salve resolve,
wrinkled little scars just one sip away
from then daft carts of not quite here / as is
an argument retch scratch in plastic veins,
lantern cups or dried flowers bent quite still
    on revenge. That wrinkle,
    is that bored floor crevice
    this class room agony?
    call it a war, where such
    as singulars is murder
to breathe, like in the air they wear their own.
A high handed cannot tickle gristles
on throats, still paved in arrears, in flip rind
pathetical weary, a we whose calm
we peel from its calamity, dreaming
what some among us could breathe like bereft
    of ties, where a scorched earth
    less easy cries, feels a clutch
    gone low wise here glazing
    long loss in dumb smile waste,
    as bile passed lathes away
    their bridge of sighs on which
my am is not, shall not nor shadow play.
This is the far cry from the comet of
politics, whose well nigh is no returned,
back from their gnostic gerundive blethers
to black colloquies of is, whose 'take' on
this is losing my rigid – there but-floors
    now beckon: a where is /
    but the moment folds, look
    how even our swan blinds

stretch, strangled in fought for
hoarse clothes, til all is of
a shudder gone, mewling
to this: *wish the life out of me* in some
possible storm where I am, luck-crust smiles
croaking artichoke hearts in mosaic
there where egg-chips splinter through *just talking*.
That wretch familiar is me, trussed in sneers,
fallow in dry-stane tears,
in all this rough cloud shower
shot to conversation
pieces, dispersing thin
precipitates, a gain
stroking their home towers
while laburnum fire is my poison friend.
Short lives, short lines perhaps too tightly drawn
for such as collapse, gob-smacked, then crisp shame
dissolving crowds in all mourning glory:
in breaks a stir too widely sawn, nor yours
then I'm not so sure all who thought is was,
but the tie, the cough, the crushing finite
when out the pin-blush tiger
or just not working bright /
never, yes not ever is
its bitter song, slapped down
as if the cream lined plum I lack were not
that kiss spit aspic in secret epic,
cash triumph in grape-pressed florid galant,
against which these star cry laments is low
plaintive screech distilled so such jaw thunder
and *really!* could not but melt privilege
to dung, even in nerve-specked destruction.
Contrary to vile appearing half-smile,
I am speechless and as wretched, growing
only such strains bizarre
as groomed burrs leech to blank

and face in utter contempt
their brute voices in soft
power, at whose larks I am only gasp;
no dialectics of mercy can stir
the stirring still or lambent ease in spleen,
only an earth flamboyant: but then, oh
how so calming seem the shattered glasses
in each several harming fall to ground, as
when conditions themselves cry out, out, or
at least bleach no more all the love I know.

A GARDEN OF TEARS

'Certain gardens are described as retreats when they are really attacks.'
                                        Ian Hamilton Finlay

I

It's a long way from love to the state we're in
here where fish are just at sea, and to know is
a law of the land, or any old wonder
as nature calls – *chuchotement* – what the dickens
can such in hope springs diurnal add up to,
or float to, so languid through these crossed channels
where spirit is without duty and knows love
for the state bliss might be when words do wither:
go then, the way of steam ships and dictators,
go then softly, quick to the ends of this life,
ineffably melding where these be pardons
and there such sacrifice is all our hatred,
stored in sand for when stones can be heard to cry
that we fear no more the heat of the trident.

II

Out that long dolour look you gave me to wean
this eldritch sadness stills the warm felt of breath
across whose cheek, and in tears, the curfew dries
as hope is salted round the lips in Gaza
stripped only so slowly to earth's hearing bone
that the face fires harsh amber from stone glances
which, once lit, extinguish this float glass plainsong,
or is it just pain in mosaic and jaw:
no, not that wish about the jowl, it is pain,

even the wall is weeping, seeping such rage
that breathing baffles, hung as a cluster of
camphire in the lost vineyards of Engedi,
where unmeasured song is suspended in brine
and barges drift, slightly stale, to the dead sea.

III

Better you to me than I were to myself
but what water we were I'm against it still,
the turn on love is patience and thousand lies
while sleepless still loves we cannot sleep still with
are breathless but still lives we cannot breathe with,
til doubt gives in fear and throws the first light stone
against names we never made, and loving break,
our breast plate of sighs in armour of accord:
call it operation bouffe, a taking leave
in lost of means, burnt islands and grimaces,
that's one end or two, a rash passion of notes
whose calm call shall remain nameless, but is law,
where wills are alive with the sound of water,
water of our eyes falling, felt and all told.

IV

The more is the pity, as to two touching,
any rainbow appears a bridge over war,
even if we do not live, nor even near,
but shuffle such as the colours of money
in the gross nets wading though this vale of tears
where an increase in size of relative debts
makes it *practically* unimaginable
that we can rely on natural forces
to stabilise our interest rates, back on track
where Zeus fuels the milky way of defence costs:
there is one other option, to allow growth

to grow and increase the critical value
of the deficit as a fraction of this
to what is, or what is still and always more.

V

Well like as maybe, the quite gentle gripe
is like as new lost, place lost in window days
where never knowingly is ever the less,
still under sold over that tread of pages
whose count me in is the harvest epaulette
and sheaves of ornamental treason; our feed
of dutiful mésalliance thinks ring on rung
as our past tense in special offers does fade,
or passes the tell by date with new freedom
to rot spontaneously: you know the rot
I mean, I take it, and savour the flavour
of its passing, into the spirit of mould
where you would love, but let the reason be love,
and just as sure as the turning of the earth.

VI

Come in the valley of the shadow of breath
where we are this kiss in impossible grief,
that never savoured wrench as now and never
when happen is, the thinking over descant
to once upon each other, folded in sums,
parts in inconstant disarray of ice
as this scream is, an only shade of dismay
that pulls each faceless tooth along to wisdom:
these are our lines upon each blowing birth bruise
dashed to lungs, as skin curls in such heavy fruit,
its lisp already for that day when one dies,

simply leaves, or forgets the flares of always,
left flickering stunned in early fear of now
when each feared for kiss is still a greater death.

VII

What not curls unknown against the lip split,
spilt quite apart from what cannot wash, and does,
as perils timid flung in held afflatus
where reason grows its only slow friend in pain
and clasps of breath fail, fall then run asunder,
spun through in what parts to remain familiar
or is the part where lightning is nothing new,
is wrung to a crush of what will not wonder:
no, and no wonder you prefer the thunder
where the piano of dull skies falls through stairs
showering air over the broken meadows
which numberless sums of all our breaking parts
even the parting past does not wish for
or cannot hold still in a pity of ears.

VIII

Count in tears through wine how it unwinding downs
out so much as a by your leaving now gone
while pleasures stretch out, bitten into the lost
something, as less of that empty slidden we
who were never this, never this in ease or
in that some kind of forgiveness for the rest,
as would remnants gather to back one's own sill
lying still among dreams there is no wish for
on such melisma drifting scars where there is,
after all, nothing natural about it:
no, not along that light flesh of which we dream

65

where tight skies are shocking to the blood of tears,
he among hers, she among his and never
but the saw in it, just this each in each saw.

IX

It's a long way still where love our gulf is war,
here where arks are royal, ripe and for sinking,
our bonds are broke, such tearing kisses, and soil
makes shifts of our futures, a water of dust
whose ashen felt rubble bursts banks on the Clyde,
where we sat down, smiled, and remembered Sion,
or was it cyanide fixed in Prussian blue
of a mind broke in fear that death becomes me,
becomes we who were what falls out together,
as perishing tears tear up the sodding earth:
for as long as the sun takes to set its gloss
the labours of our loss are still glistening,
and where the going is over, gone over,
there we go, slightly pale, to the ends of love.

FOUL PAPERS

'Reading the morning newspaper is the realist's morning prayer. One orients one's attitude towards the world either by God or by what the world is. The former gives as much security as the latter, in that one knows how one stands.'

G. W. F. Hegel

Clamour for change, with this to plough on
even though fresh mint, under a flat
climate, borders on wisteria
buoyed and flushed in a slogan too far,
or wills no attempt to portray what palls
as in every body flirts, don't they?
So minting, some feel like death over it
whose only sin is unlikely grist,
wit and wag this sizzling raunch bears all,
wailing wall to boot, and now we're told
due more to Herod's engineering,
nature not withstanding, as a fly
passes on withering western winds,
and all the bold sedge goes hand in fist,
spent in forage round other and earth.

Clamour not least, past swift dilation
for azure foul papers in sweet play
of wild water, the feather that broke
the duck's back, dipped in pools of ready
honey, debit where debit is due,
a base rate cut to the plucked bone,
pitted out in rigid crumple zones
as seams have been sunk since Hadrian.
We thank our lucky stars and revise
the data on kills and blue ribands,
as water bleeds its bracelet of salt,

worth its weight in hands, and now we're told
shaking gold cut fingers, marine silk
that speaks of handless baby clusters
as hushed surfactants quite safely graze.

Clamour still, as you would read the wash
based on dark loads and average soiling
singing loss gone awol, a green fudge
of nod, wink and blister, such dry rot
huffing that, we are told, is frankly
a doddle, till the dam breaks and beans
spill from the land of cash injection.
Gone to blazes and dipped in envoys,
the rank agents whose colours are fast
go tender to the touch of order
and tough it out amid charcoal clouds,
as terms refer to the bags of bones
in bland agitation, rumour washed
articles without finish or likeness
whose effluence fills our pale and seas.

Clamour from the names, whose cloudy cast
faces air strikes from the seraphim
up on high, while this little piggy
goes a gambol on serotonin
and molochs are off as the fly crows,
forever a risk in the mind's ear,
whose dogs are present feeding frenzy
which is not pretty, but makes hot news
off the top rack, then back to my place
for a flurry of front page gloire
and nemesis time on the footsie,
while ten thousand chickens died, we're told,
in a fire started on purpose, though
I suppose it's the marine in me
says go if the hearing continues.

Clamour for addicts, alive in sticks
of fax affairs and first eruption
through glimpses of cleft and labia,
while poor old sterling is under weight
on a hike in prices, and under
a weather which can't be taken in
or sitting down, while for our next dish
it's double or quits, hip, hip, who spat
such off piste sleaze and in arms parade
a dose of thorp, or tamoxifen
blown hot and bold, moggies to a man
in mordent fervour, the air on strike
over plateau and reed beds of risk
as blue print turns sage, but can still feel
for how the grey suit sticks to each skin.

Clamour no more, for a deal of dove
gone sky wire, our oiled palms find hardware
more soft than the belly has hot airs,
and in chilled stunts are first on, then off,
their baying hounds set on upbeat calls
for coarse customs, and in no such hint
go dark if the picture recovers,
or talk up a hobble on tax hikes
to pick me up, such fiscal tigers
taming their flock with rock and new gall,
while in concrete and clay, trial by fire
is the here and now, back on bunkers
going for a swan song, as calls go up
singing blue is the colour and bull
is the name of the game in soft gold.

Clamour on one eye, single-minded
nor ever shall be, word without bend
in a maze of blight, such flush jobs are
water, the pool of unemployment

in snug duvet, as snowy the dog
sniffs out or swims in insolvency,
clever genes gone fuck about, with swabs
dipped in the big E, our winning mix
of gin and pork, oh yes we do lead
a charmed life, in a dignity pack
with soapy truth brush steeped in shut traps
amid the splendid male voice choir,
now lurching in green sprouts, so we're told,
or at least crippled by scree rapture
is cheek by jowl in open crimson.

Clamour calling, its bolts from the blue
rhumba, and we'll be your base data
if you'll be our super structure, sun
in angry litters, all pants to play
then gammy tykes, with dicks in the dock
or is there no end to the dam clouds
on tinderbox, as the air strikes through.
Excuse us, tyroes of the heat sky
as the gravy train chunders up stream,
though one hundred thousand sea-birds die
from want of food, rapid razor-bills
turned over, done for in silent spring
or wind glows of hush now, such muffin
and gruel throws sol-fa on soft country,
up with which this will not put, or kiss.

Clamour on the nose, and a head start
burning for suck and booty, or flags
in cobalt package, a whole peace hog
of ripped chords and fresh motor neurones,
their pert bonds jumping over dam busts
and heaving blondes feeling tit for tat,
while today, we're told, a young man died
of chicken pox and one party rule,

and despite new poll blows for tigers,
a firm pact of tough flesh goes on peps
and prosper, as flagging glands on ice
stage a late rally on the index
with the bad news priced in, a good thing
going, just like that, from solid snogs
to old mother thorp and brass dogma.

Clamour and welter, bearing in mind
what passes for mood in high-rise riffs,
hot core norms blowing in on coming
storm clouds, agog with fair sex, fair deal,
as square goes is the nobble and dance
turning in on fine de sickle sheets,
these watery beds of lost leaders,
these droll thickets gone sidereal.
You wish it were all a fast caper
of bounty and bright bunting, not this
too deaf and fuzzy circuit, Venus
and filo pastry, now arc-welding
for all its worth like the day is long,
and though buffs disagree, it is best
to save the killer routine to last.

Clamour to put off on a brave face,
the suds of the day are blowing home
to heat up the candid, all that phew
just soaking up a few salad rays
on savage humbug, you know how sums
go lumpy, their string vests and interests
swanning along with saints and sham rock,
if you catch my rift or sweet chassis.
But I don't suppose the day is young
as the clock stops on a new record
and fear takes the biscuit, hope the bronze,
then mortar the sheen, now mouthing off

to solid tips, like there's little point
in a title that can't sit pretty
on the lips of the target market.

Clamour that keeps on coming, as hawks
and wind scales just hang fire over head
then go vamoose, burning up a head
of double gold, glands on overdrive,
while bad apples rot and our lost lines
beef up on sad cow and sunken face,
such engaging bursts of pink candour
in frank millstones, or codpiece and gulp.
But as mites set out to bite the dust,
the promise of more spectaculars
rings a dirge, and the power of plastic
touches things you touch without thinking,
so let's not be picky, hold on for now,
stand toxic, tall and tousled, as we
go forth coldly into the dark page.

HOW PEACE CAME

if I may be so bold
or night evince
go suck on tip of sour tongue and come in
into the red
on purple drum and drag
chained to blown organs of good old Corti
or casus belli on Balkan toast
saying blast! deafness!

the chair is still triste hélas
and a plague on all your roses
your soft pate
and dome

come into the red
here where crabs are so dishy
amid rouge stripes slow firing
amber mouton rage
lip lash expresso
pressed citrons crying Papa!
ou fuck that for a laugh Clio
as the cute muse wears mud and cucumber glasses
bidet on brioche
e-mail mousse setting rust on angel delight

for Paul Klee

*

the problem of sonic boom is now clearly
                        upon us
                                and in spades
                        but if I may be so cold
                                        let's rip chords
                from a priori harp rooms
and staunch the ripe flow of steady eddies
        these king-size ears in eau de calumny
                                born to backsheesh
for the bloody boom forms a high carpet
                and dry cotton
        affords no protection

                        no, and no red ripple to come into
which is about as much as we can take
                                bars in our eyes
                                stars in our hearts
                        and holes on fur
                as the chevalier d'industrie
                                green king on ice
        says go and catch a falling plate

and in whipped dreams I'm afraid
                                for kindred spirits
                or who would play savage rumpus
                                on tap

                                *

                        it's a gas at any rate
                in one take and in the can
                                dido and dada for the under fives
        braggadocio in sublime dough
listless myopics to can the noise
                a keep down low and rank

74

piquant flowers on plasticine park
                            sucking punter's lisp
        in art thou heavy breathing
                or just good friends
                      or better still?

                no matter no mufti
        we're on the wing for sure
                if you'll join us
and no place like the better part at bay
            so bank on it buddy
till greater pressures force the tube wide open
        gales in tiny tots
            where dank white trash is hurt neon
            like laughter
            and we take the air
        or more simply fail to swallow
            the gall

*

if I may be so sounded
        come off it
        capital is not late
        nor mature
      nor a higher plant than the weed
        it just grows on you
leaves of paper notes fluttering
        in the annex
        and bonds booming
        in ah, ah domine deus
        we're here for the duration
            suits in clubs
and thanks for having us
                the food was rude

so how about it
a peace of action
feet in drag down the path
amid red quakes of crazed paving

mandibles just ajar
chin up in Mary's garden

and yer must be kidding
it will never do
what with the insurance
and all hell to pay
not counting corpses under the grill
mine's a burger
with en suite sauce

*

back on the warm sonant front
            war weariness is all the rage
a truce for sore ears

what serene candy

melts a stern areopagus to butter
        gold capped teeth
who need mastic like a hold in the head

their standing armies
gone right to the mirth's surface
lank curlews struck dumb
a sluice passing ports
gin slings
then fizzy bombs

kindly wipe your feet on my soul
before you come in
into the red
from coccyx to cochlea
where glow notes go
and more privy in the bush than on a vice hand
shaken to its ends
dust bowls rung on bugger all gongs
pity as pap says
· the world's not a fair race
so give over
if I may be so old

*

all aboard!
once bitten twice blithe
rouble-breasted spirit!
you have so many ways of drinking us
to the lees
but is that Europe in your package
or are you just pleased to fleece us Jason?

deep fangs sunk in legoverland
going like a dump trunk
a melt down
mars in vice
for we are the way we go to it

get artic'late baby
there's a super highway passing through you
don't be a nimby
not in my black yarn
cuss cup and garrotted
in worsted threads of axle grease
and thimble

hey asda!
you're a plonker
grunging the motorcade
or blocking soft lows and beta
that's Alph
liminal wet stuff
and hooded grace

*

will someone tell that tambourine man
to turn it down?

it's more than flesch can bare its brass to

a ray fawning
in brash diamante glory
we can't hear ourselves blink
for open neck sweaters and bream
the heart rackets and rattle cries
of Eat Gucci!
bowl and cowl and gore
now the hail is hard as
meat balls

ah bisto
what's cooking Titus?
sock it to me like you do
on tusk and tiramé su
oh move over soft now lady
or they'll love you to death

which reminds me
fancy taking a king's soggy biscuit?

cool tank tops with Scottish widows
man, the gear's terrific
such a blooming dark habit
becomes you

*

as sky falls into global muff
wrapped around in melanin tans
in fax of fuzz box
there's mud in your lie

are you feared of creatures
such as that slunk yawn
of art thou slow dancing

unprepared to leave space for air
beneath the flow of bodies
whisked to viper
for the hair you breathe
clasping your untipped
furry tongue

no way no snake bite
just forked tongue
on doggy brek
get that down you
pic 'n' mix herbaceous borders
freshed off Balkan smorgasbord
oh but it does you good to go suck tartan
weight off your pins
as the clutch goes off the risus purus
chocs and spleen away
countdown and left off!
to the end of our
common era

*

dinosaurs are us
stuff the red commie peppers
go into black vests
it's all the rage
a quote sir?
'you can't run a revolution in a suit and tie'
yeah I hear what you're braying
pornocrat sud
go blonde lagoon
hoppit Scotch git
marg wouldn't melt on your silver tonsils
or moss pap
just suck it and see

the mint with the cold war in the middle
is where the bucks stop
def minky and jaws
fin-soup or arch culls
though the ecu in your hand is worth
all the rosey gun teeth and dripping

such hard lard
felt old
consistency of flesch
soft to burn

but dad, what's the moon meant to
advertise? and can I have some
for afters

*

no way no beagle bender
up the wall and over the counter

we'll see seams of rags
in stitches
barely visible
from our seat here among falling clouds
in gambolling amber dawns

it's a barking ballet
it's a ballroom blitz

pssst!
wanna buy a bazooka?
fresh out of spinach pyjamas
but there's a war in the ice-box
if you need a pick-me-up

it's d.i.y.
as sky falls off cusps of rust
off such able arms of worm
and into a sump
round pegs in bauble sulk
done to touch paper sheen
the lit earth still humming
zephyrs blown to a floss

the stars so starry
howling arf arf bauhaus

oh Thermidor

BENCH MARKS

'In short we retreat into the selfishness that stands on the quiet shore, and thence enjoys in safety the distant spectacle of "wrecks confusedly hurled". But even regarding history as the slaughter-bench at which the happiness of peoples, the wisdom of states, and the virtue of individuals have been victimized—the question involuntarily arises—to what principle, to what final aim these enormous sacrifices have been offered.'

G. W. F. Hegel

1 CARTE BLANCHE

Be out of this ear shot
to a least spirit level,
shaking rag hands off
through silvery vibrato
or bone shed languish
to quid whistle, where
languish suggests a rustle
and there is none nor rime.

Or where hot and like is
something like a silence
gone, no buts but brio in
spins, swaddling by dint
of soft ruse, so still calls
what won't bear thinking
on, wrung the way we
blur to hollowed timbre.

What burning crumbles,
what a sharing place and
what simples to indulge,
there's the rub, spirit chaff,
a half line of rack tissue
for the longueurs, for the
traceries of warmth, for
dust on graceless needle.

Slipper top of dazed shots
with no tain, sour preserves
to the lever where ore,
no doubt, is scratch placid,
the stir crazies row on
like this life depends, or
with no wish wash, only
trade winds & funk qualms.

Leave off to join the stir,
lip to this swift carpet
on siren audit, ear run
aground, what sleet rumbles
do lanky mire, wheat pools,
polls of grim reserve turning
a blind why, would you not
bury this, my soft head?

Nor want of cris de cœur,
a turn, two half hitches
rounded up to this near
prospect of belated watch,
hush money, what a haar
mouth gives, a far verge
proffers island semeion,
hard prest count me outs.

Dextrorse aromas burn
sky high off acid wits,
we're not in good odour
you and I, nor fit for the
patience of piecemeal
latinity, dog eat dog or
slow barques to rhodes,
you cannot be serious.

Jump ship, blow sanguine,
rheum over slavish oils,
creole brushed doldrums
dipping scurf print in surf,
just get on swimmingly,
sere as siroc winds scratch
green backs, blood welter
in desert schwärmerei.

Scat happy, lax, rope burn
from chord nave to pinion,
cut to ribbons, club class
torpor shanghaied by deaf
stringers, dead cert penny
will drop, back to pieces,
inch fickle for hard slog,
the bit between high jaws.

Once horizons, scalp bland
in serried auction, boil
cosy, o cane the rind,
this serif in lashings,
smoke as homing salmon
up glove fits, bell temper,
vicious circles cut scoff
or some scald soon spent.

Bone dry and willow, an
oriflamme wash, zip high
in armour heels, no slip
o the wisp, as it were,
imprest on idle ashes,
ripe flesh and still ash,
pentose, blossoming in
puce cracks, the flute burns.

Hues of resolve but not
your kind, o worse tone
done to felt dross, a whey
of antimony, cauchemar
and junk, you don't give
a bald fig for worm bast,
for silky guts, colewort
twice sodden and bitter.

Nor do you give a pursed
lip, not for all the bumf
pneuma and piped lilies
in red peril, cold ochre
turned pale, a slow rout,
a light cast of chenille,
ivory bars and parchment,
what wouldn't you give?

So in a silk kiln, for
want of a better shine
and as spun dry o vast
of burning arras, purse
larva, aeolian harps and
parched skies, o give
me a dossil for this,
give me a slipper name.

Then a beating rots still,
a nodus, noose in flame
shrub to imagine with
or go down a velvet
storm, a rude hint of
rouble and cherry stone,
each groan on the tapis
before smiling obloquy.

Sweet shift go slow, go
amid shingle and roc
and be so the camera
lies in felt ice, in harm,
a brim too far, a maw
in litotes, our gorge
simply rises, comes to
to this general striking.

Or to some skurried bell,
sops a drift, democrats
in coup de main, row on
row and all for no one's
wedding, o dead rose
what murrain soldering
choler to fruits of gloom,
title tracks, this livid soil.

A cold comes in from
the links, sing of no
it will not do and then
is policy, from polder
to dry land, that's all
folks, now the labour is
in creels, gross lobster
to boil a living pink.

A scratch, a half moon,
pad on nail as you do,
out of sorts with party
hats, the heart eaten in
to marrow, o liquid
assets, dog days on the
verge, a bleeding marge,
a mount of crimson ease.

So go easy on the eye
above in fetid stars of
topic balm, high spirits
and cold accord of ruth,
sweet tigers, splash out,
your days melt in surds,
a fair and each to each
to the tune of millions.

A mandate bitter fills
in weighty shoes, but
count me out, as I say,
or fast in to this span
of harm, o give me
breaking part to play,
the good going, salver
cup, truss, beauty asp.

Then again, maybe not,
no creature lung to glean
off bile as leaking bones
do folly in granite ire,
so clasp thorns, a clasp
and glimmer in thermal
glottis, shape o foxy
to a dark, coke cologne.

The char is on, each to
bungle under spar hat
where tides give way, a
ruse spangles, a fine silt
unhappens as you throng
off kilter, see in streaks
of open pit, surging slag,
draff to radium arbors.

Window dress, a wound
in drip gavage, o torch
to dry docks, cicatrice
where the army passes,
but scales vermilion, if
in glows do gala flares
on onions of shut eye,
such schism in murmurs.

A strike is on, o sacred
and violable, in sullen
massing, staunch hush
in wings so mar cloudy
that long rain fills with
a lethal breath, a stake
in cool elective intrigue
or a stake in sad news.

Show me, palsied arm
whose glance lightens
afar, no more a whirl
on wastes of war, on
ship of hope, surprise
and otter, as a nymph
to irresistible emerald
and one eye shot out.

Bring me another pot
of sanguine fire, ditto
on flowered and fancy
goods of sundry kinds,
so demoralised by dole
and frame, what wrecks
in girth of central sinks,
this full, so torpid state.

At hazard of our lives
go stop the one, shut
the other, sly spirit of
thrushgrove among us
who will but ill apply,
as comes to scoff but
remains to pray, deaf
to beady stuff of idols.

Wild rose nor old man's
beard, rambling on, nor
may, blackthorn blossom
to quickset hedge, clipped
so low in bonds of peat,
well moulding, for you
to cease to be, o worms
for her proud to tread on.

Take a chopin of soup,
a scone a day, whiles
fasting, whiles getting
meat, at a squeeze, so
to drops, so democrat
bloody, factions cut to
your every throat, but
here you are no relief.

Still blaze, sooty rabble,
vile nebs and base rads,
a throw of radical clegs
falling, prog in the guts
again, now levelling on
a blaze of sable trains,
which can but laugh or
make over in its image.

What lies on mutilated
frame, our muted spits
to purest flame, calm
as ever apparatus gone
to seed, scaffold song
collects in soon ranks
unsubdued, sing iron
gasp now to red wash.

The blue of the eyes is
never so clear as now,
in blind hands born to
bandage, plasters, each
map on vellum, a fringe
of sheperd moon, gone
to bleed, a braided spot
of bother so cancerous.

A torn rigging, mast of
splitters clears out your
poor cape to warm voice,
so come now, blood sea
between us, sore guilds
in rises and flow charts,
what last straw can cling
to such verges of amber.

Folded fault go hither
in plane of weakness,
crusts of spine til our
suitable host, a shear
zone, fills a deep seat
in open conduit, steep
to dip as a quartz vein,
each of cut off grades.

Sling off a yoke turgid
so bitter spun on fizzy
pills, spears and axes,
pressed in soubriquets
worn to stagnant pools,
or just one more titanic
work to rue, that solar
flare sticks in the craw.

2 AGGROPOLIS

Rampart of early kin
gdom, lamp hand can
no more surly, but as
worsted lands decry to
most governable parcel,
as to wold civil squall
aurochs abound in not
them as wont, carse noy.

Thane & carls & carline
willing able fief reivers,
rangers of their dogger
lone crust to derby stars,

so vassal span to glass
in minor modes, what
diffuse trickles burn own
grands off of apex argot.

Arrant? I nearly lost my
half heid shantil shining
though the lame is way,
which than mune is worth,
bang clannish as but kin
could no more grip fringe
than teeth rankles mak a
moment too too cramasay.

Coronach the mak undid
in cordial griddle burns,
a sack of sword firing to
a river's rough wooing,
so tending extremities
whereunto ye may reach
ample scarcement, fuse
crux to steelbow now.

This too, too barren pit
y gallows, rough shod
rise do plunge back all,
semper strong to bake
o local magnate, corbie
conner, flox, manrents,
a chisel home none durst
taste so striving sunders.

But from our throat band
each one to boaster skull,
a whole brood bought and
sold for some quiet death,

there native shafts to serf
through keen run pestilence,
a third off all churl, a dirt
canker of lank blown land.

Exceeding cruel, mingle
speir hemmed in to style
as a boot on other foot
loose felt a margret rose,
a taxi, mum, what wedge
there calling asserts its
ainmaist equilibrium as
a fringe now all to burn.

Back a hammer lens do
great jessie smithereens
to bolster bless arraign,
not prickle state of mars
in ready armour wards,
auld antonine crumbles
haps in rage to ditches
farflung een to danzig.

Renegades saw broke
men go, the going is
sure primogeniture to
a trace of shedding so
seldom sacked in old
sense or auld kail dosh,
said but spelt like read
lays never said fer awe.

Negleck nocht but to flee
curls oer seas, oer muling
chiel clock, the never ripe,
that seat of learning curve

to whey & splinter grey,
vehement against idols,
caw, caw mid a grave, a
set fair but for the grace.

Brethren mort dues cure
soul fonts, hook & crook,
a took fire noblesse oblige,
piety so mother smothered
in wanton cloth dochters
to seed a tipping bath but
whipped up rabble beefy
gin bondage of strangers.

Largely dead letters shine
heretic forth & kale stunt,
bell bent on fleeter dash,
as caress but tools o rift
to sun amok gaunt cries
as jasus and no quarter,
severed sore, a rip stone
to flounders blue in print.

Thorns out of pulpit be
the luggis lurid knuckle,
pillory and darling dross
under vane and fruitful
stool, fouls no flesh but
durst no pool of handfast
where but sent fine section
shocks fall, wave or crow.

Wish art burns a stake,
owl to dawning oar, so
little prophets its gale,
galley dusk welt scarry,

civil rapture & salve tar
to jeopard lives in ash,
heart singing apostatic,
a force of law, a mass.

Doth corn among chaff
rest except thou repent,
o monstiferous empire,
we espy not the flame,
decks above thy skin
coats death did so enter,
ensign chant of circe
in thy hot displeasure.

Linen & skins ring back
a swell pitch to mix some
shewe of civilitie, these
other alluterlie barbares,
no civil plant in roomes,
sic colonists then drive
a wedge between celts,
kintyre bludie to antrim.

Clamp fro plangent isle
to plantation of ulster,
laity tree carbon bound,
as thou o lord onely art
deservedly more master
than my sel, who would
had lesse been affected
in irelands & sad estate.

Gall vinegar of falsity
and contempt with the
cups of my affliction,
cyclopick monster as

fears utter extirpation,
tenants in battle array,
true banditti reappearing,
barrel o brandy on staff.

Beyond a head dyke, all
as round a rough bone,
rig torn so weedy baulk,
neer moves a mountain
diffuse in clachan haze,
seeks oatfowl eenbright,
pristine mid light wattle
going to but blank stane.

Struck dearth murrain so
to blooding the laird's ky,
visage scorn, as for want
some die, a wayside flux
shifts its flaming ague,
plague in a white cloud,
flea daunce o black rat
lays on of partly waste.

Glade poverty turns light,
stood on brink of great
jenny & water frame &
mule & throstle carding
engines gin scurvy blest,
potato mirth akindling,
a cruel havoc dauncing
thro kail & leaf & croup.

Marks of tide, a radical
wash hung liberty high,
dreg silver in our cups
as no sanguine rabble,

no sir, nor a down tool
to turkey-red dyes, tar
to coal, naphtha starch
wearing veins of jasper.

Canals into the drill of
the lag, rolls so rent to
cast transplants, stook
bitter on summit entails
their tapering heads do
cut and turn, flail sabre
in shag dragoons, your
virgin heart so burning.

What a way to cast clods
on kindred spirits, there
the sulk is on, you take it
all in, and chew mildew
like there's no wake left
and no worm, each head
of jawfall in calm lore as
so forth serries this waif.

But hither, crash viol,
the loose twang in gas
and halter, its sermon
ever falters, never no
fine tooth in sundries,
schmo labrets, there's
hurt to your elbow, so
gone on open mouths.

The taint of the carving
is in the slummy blood
of what grows feebler
in sulky grace, miasma

riding over, getting out
while the going is bad,
so less of that colossal
cheek & maiming sou.

Stark & stacked so bitter,
what crocks of shedding
on a tide of nails, pins,
even to base metals and
no end of toil, no don't
go on, leave off, hunger
to a rage, buried in bone
shackle to palpable scar.

Worse is come under in
inclement skies, before
each dark spit takes you
to water felt upon awes,
dusts down in pig iron,
swan of arc-light, flock
done to sparry feather,
ember gorse in dolefuls.

In wet soil, crisp white
scale holds to its mire,
what drip stalks, such
cut swathes, the rumble
slump and insert larks,
its best lie deep, steady,
the number dogs do lay
a dirt trail in each script.

Blue moon on fed day,
smiles so still, or soon
dies, drops a halo, hot
suits of nuclear electric

on th'ensanguined suns,
garb o grime, in rails of
bleached bondehede, no
ash of its worth or page.

O fucked city, its agon
lustre in foamy rind, to
do so soft with then on
acrylic afternoons, our
one good eye flowering
me with disaffections,
ah mine hurt, it shrinks
from less, it shrugs on.

As bake or dearth into
star cot, let's lie lower
love, let's lie low until
no dark so comfortless
blight of agent can still
wager head aginst our
rotting core, as they do
expatiate of this or fall.

Have you left my ear to
locks, a field of night in
the mine, ivresse as this
hair kindles into meteor
or blows of die, a mark
as fur or as sark blisters
rent asunder, its moral
streaks in fiery blesses.

So flower the baby for
pure boot and spur, to
list with zeal on banner
sky, each bright light is

you, for the taking, our
surfing oxide, treats of
burnished ore, its civil
song so shiney in wax.

You stand on a floor
of noise, its broken
vessels turning to a
savage lavender, the
soles flying through,
as so stuns a face to
unfold in each nerve,
each slice that carves.

In strokes or gritted
hate, its proud beats
to your darker pulp,
so steer a stern, clear
out this dormant sky,
now so cool or crost,
and cut a dash, esprit
doux, out of all cry.

3 OPTIC FIRE

Drop off of curtains
sleepless, so torn to
pale coats of acid lid,
the bends or spumes
up in optic fire, flesh
still pressed to trysts
of laburnum, arc of
our cuffs in poison.

Or shimmer through
its velvet clasp, each
torso unfurled where
beams recoil, where
feathered rage drives
glass slivers through
a wide frown, beads
upon beads of harm.

Glory be its darkest
drop, come dark to
dog's tail in flaring
redoubt, come lime
to ensnare a pigeon
fancier, sweet meats
or crusts, silver tops
or nectar all the way.

Nor fresh of breath
air, nor flavours of
the hour, no sloosh
to tattery twinklings
where the eye folds
over, save a limbus
of vanity, rosa solis
gone frail in graphs.

Blush upon ire, this
racing lark no aging
creeper, nor reason
no, but brush, how
can you not, how as
but cynic winds give
good, go ache then,
take our feebleness.

Slip into this caress
of nomination, just
in you, as a burning
child dreads the fire,
leopard slur hanging
in landings, til sleep
comes down, comes
to or boots up silver.

This aching eye bent
to decay, grass of flat
hill, streaks for dusk
wreaths as sparrows,
felt chin in felt hand,
a call of wild boy or
such feasts on shell,
on scripts at anchor.

Fields blow out of all
semblance, bled gums
whimper for flocks in
rickets, each their own
screen as we total out
of sympathy, whisper
to new emulsion, ever
eager for why we fail.

Severed ears, you offer
no par value in flowing
shares, shade specious
to redeem a pro forma
base, sunk to reflect on
new reserve, lit ounces
in stripping nets, your
orebody done to length.

Then turn your so avid
eyes to ripple, neckline
cricked to flint, elbows
done to oil or so down
in the mouth, as where
they leave you to gape,
deliquescent, fontanelle
or not, you dip and dye.

Or eyes still dwell on
dark exterior, shades
who would eat each
other sown in bacillus
tread, this stark house
of cash, silver weeds,
riot grain wrapped in
splints or fulgent cot.

Still as dead hands, a
poise on the brink of
hydro tears, a future
for hot moss moves
as each asking price
cracks the whip, but
will not bear up, nor
wait up much longer.

For no sake, nor tops
of heat, architrave for
a flat, pale face, who
you do not grieve for
but mouth blank spots
to thousand lintels or
sprouting casts, cave
of this its heavy ache.

Set freedom by storm,
livery shy, mope eyed
by living so long in
hab nab, whetstone or
mizzle, it's one to me,
death's arquebuse or
punch sore, but take
me for an open sword.

Wise behind the hand,
her fresh pucker would
aroint thee skein dazzle
on rings of one finger,
jade glint as shepherds
gently burn, hysteresis
as heimat burns, drops
off in chats we are not.

Back to blight, a blush
flares and cast of zeal,
cut swabs to red falx,
dura mater, umbrage
and rankle, what shale
fanfarades so choke to
round, turns to coulisse
for a sake still, even so.

Pirouette, what a glaze
to show, sunk field of
lace net, odso, come
doxy, were you burnt
to cinder or torn up in
such hush and brogue,
gifts as broom yields
honey in her smiling.

The hat fits, would you
but know it, œillade and
bone dropsy hacked on
to temples, we're clean
through, couleur de rose
and brackish, ah, cool
sulcus, simmer free of
its maths in sultry yarns.

Bereft, put a cold front
in mood swings, curve
or cut legs to the quick,
scissile, at any rate, or
a goner, so sash keen,
scampy and hale, better
late ripe and bare than
blossom or umber blast.

Each to each, the braid
irks, fathomless in rank
peonage, chip in, drop
lustre, o barbed chaff,
your brim flows on as
feet go blow by blow,
stiller than a rude grant,
a cut price in demijour.

What a palaver, fond as
a drifting besom, fasces
and bengaline ripped to
shreds, let the dust off
soles, a wash and gape
before you go, and then
in one fell swoop the fall
over the baresark moon.

Its night is young, you
doubt it, but over cast
go staunch in diploma,
rod to leaking spine, so
dirigent waves her rank
to wove of pitchblende,
all as unsewn plateaux,
skin, bone and armour.

But as shatter gusts of
fresher air, what starch
holds out palp resolve,
a mote or curn, it goes
without saying, it turns
nasty before your very
iris, its glance of paste
worn as words fail me.

Felt in transient beam,
as the more near alike
the more neat the kiss
change, you take our
breath away, steeped
in curves, burns full
for source traits to do
no chromosome flame.

Worse still, no starter
bust to wreck but our
platinum shade, none
the wiser, quaverings
in such heaviness for
what can't be caught
in immanence, faces
turning to some wall.

Pour on, or mould to
a ruin this stream for
fear, such cloud foes
of red, a magnet to its
dim pouts, set distant
from what slips off in
the midst as the paper
still holds out for less.

Star after star, army
of pale fleece, turn a
fiery crest in this hue
or temper as its heap
slides a berry whose
spine lies broke, one
half ripe, for lush lip
as her nom de plume.

Were it to be wished,
no wreath but curves
in strange kind, your
silly meadow corner,
that stench of the lab
and the gray woof of
her as she falls, gross
per long wave mould.

A cloud of happy, o
can perhaps this deal
cut less to pale down
as she haunts the air
or courts her smiling
lawn, a voice of the
light, as at least this
light and fierce draft.

So cold, rigid child
à ras de terre, done
by sort or tacit curls
to a screen of stops,
pallid shades, varied
as they are cruel, for
angry knots so flaring
off in chilly grounds.

Each hue spelt a far
warm, dust buds of
spleen all bled with
rapport that takes its
shelter from a comet
in acrylic ochre, idle
in realms of briar so
gives the eye to brine.

In gradient scream, a
shallow ash, so brisk
to pierce each glassy
foam, casts its slouch
posture to dimities of
blue, a fall from nets
to surf flats, a sugar
to still such revulsion.

So give up the ghost
then, lay off its laws
or want of better for
a want of we in your
mind's eye, nor love
to unfurl through all
this immune system
laying down its arm.

Eat out of heart, turn
baroque soma, pulls
to threads where the
bosom sways its age
in blue hued moons,
each gives out, so let
me conclude, a tinted
wreck for a rest of it.

You're all ears, or say
so, flushed at what to
see through each ruse,
my emphasis, as slop
head of brook, burn,
glittering swim, or all
that, orbits of hate in
glows, now go proxy.

Out of a proud band
your pallor goes to a
sheen, gives me lark
city and death, I am
frankly appalled, pale
as freak rivers to this
shock of how long it
takes, just how long.

4 HIGH TIME

As to take a morn eye
in every sense, out of
soughing air, do that,
moiré cough and acrid

yawn, what charm its
going has, each bland
quip and simper, now
that's what I call hush.

Of violet and neurosis
there liquid banks into
lemon or velvet, forget
which, such a cabbage
or sassafras flare, here
an income policy, there
a sweet scent of causes
lost in buckets of light.

So preened go votives
to motto oil, mix well
and feel this cleavage
before a fresh libation
commences its grease
parade, caterwauls in
suburbs of their proxy
heart, my flesh crawls.

This body of work, the
sordid do in inner surf,
where does its caravan
of fur get off, the skin
in tremors of static, so
freshly cut, spasms of
apricot heats to fill out
forms for luxury pains.

It is so sweet, sherbet
throat, black dabs on
dorsal horns, larks of
its hired hand done to

defile even cool napes
such as yours, or rage
parked behind a desk,
but not worth its salt.

Three bones press fluid
to sweeps and triggers,
operation shut up shop
breaks heavy air to the
merchant army, so blue
in denture and claw, its
bloody veil, or a jaguar
of laughing right angles.

Our betters propose a
picnic, sprays of bitter
pills, what salty melon
spread over a surface
dying of brass tongue,
the mucous slab cut to
craving muscle or gone
to blaze for an instant.

A star burst, a harvest
in glass fathoms blown
to this, purple trains of
antique oral crusts, no
kidding, even sabers of
pure ideology across a
night fire, it smoulders
so and perishes in glitz.

Money slipper, a spice
so suffuses the sky of
abstract quantity that
mirth fills the evening

gall, its family breezes
loosening myelin fibre
with carping traces to
give each other the lie.

But not so much give
as what will you sink,
so gilds this pill, what
ground states or level
of resonance, on a sill
quite silver with each
passing brilliance, its
energy in bitter ends.

Yours to certain harm,
breadth of glance, not
such to set a burnt orb
on industrial pickle, or
such as the worst case,
but our very own, fist
over ornament, hand in
teeth, so hold me tight.

We pass at once to the
fist of names, a course
of sneers, gilding rust
of acid auroras, this is
for you, I try to suffer
better, then less, gone
on convictions, there's
no need for it, no wish.

As her physic so wins
and its luminous crop
is so fast, what pulls a
regard along like this,

which brow searches
their lining, that flight
of fact, don't make me
a smile nor even glow.

The recovered falls or
turning parts, each to
spare their blush, but
might not some sordid
pearl hang on intrinsic
determination, a swift
go to a red flex, what
flesh just left it saying.

Or such is its armature
for rainy days, its drop
much like another, you
lend an eye, then find
the distributive process
quite lacking in refined
calm, no more domestic
than a moral landscape.

Not bitter on the choke
as its certain finesse of
symptom purity, but a
sour take, a face to the
bowls of mime, moist
sheen flaring, locked in
pale schemata so liquid
flows out this open rim.

A lesion in this central
region, while yet more
motes and atoms hold,
the day up in arms, as

its strong, even stroke
evokes no tonic reflex,
not even a rose ring of
blood around this bath.

On no account, and on
no more does this skin
rest its vigil, cherished
as the organism abides
by a loved constitution,
just not the ticket, cares
needled behind bars for
a broken stick of party.

Much frayed at the edge
then, a human element
growls its militant last
ditch, their tendency to
yet finer points of open
face, saline revels, more
the merrier, rumbles or
wished still for hissing.

So come away, free as
a vital organ, a courtly
mouth now palm high
in arbitrage, play this
zest or minimum wage
to cool sops or broken
spine, the buds of sage
spent on only one day.

You take it all back, all
you ever ran through,
from frosted silver foil
to the spitting curls of

piping hot camouflage,
such fighting talk, here
where not one whiff of
rank child is left to air.

On hedges now down
at heel, go along fierce
gardens, feel gears up
for a major assault on
the welfare, one sweet
missive after another,
done to scale on scarp
carbons, nunc dimittis.

This cold side of habit
transfers, you pan and
scan for scrags, a gram
of flesh, cut to mantles
still incident on its thick
tape, sparky frostwork
holding out quick films
of nightly stupefaction.

Yes, that's the spirit, go
flatter a wilderness into
a fossile dawn, sleek as
from a certain red, find
some arc of dread, livid
with emphasis, nostrels
set to stun, each a danse
of drops laid out so low.

Leave off, before belts
of straw do their death
rattle, keep the skin on
each tooth, just rest up

on bloody minded sail
or claw, this flood has
no end in sight, this is
your local opportunity.

Smiles of salt in shared
wounds, why settle for
less, why miss the rug
doctor rental system at
its level best, you play
some part of demolition
so let sorrow unfurl in
each well earned glory.

Harbour lung, the gash
come to falter, a chiasm
even as bulbs burst into
savage integument, even
as that rag doll rots, just
0.3mg short of opening
fury, what arcs along its
shifting tread and shade.

Still, its specific charge
burns through, held on
thrown reliefs, to walk
upon some broken cart
on juice, to do its drail
upon over-cooked stag
fleece, across a prosaic
clutch of dormant plant.

No point in harking or
come hard knit brows
into plunging fogs of
low droop, decked in

hoots which slope off
into mobile sucklings,
these ganglion nuclei,
their blooming fumes.

Nor even a last laugh
where a case of easy
cuddles, that shudder
of, say, the fish head
in collects of hand to
mouth, ends on bent
knees, its dead simple
ligature of gored lace.

So reek to high havoc,
our wild use numbers
flow bland, wrecks in
aggregates, equipment
so full for the duration
on smatterings, a sere
bulk of data, bone high
and laid out opal bales.

Fly me to our room of
least computed mocks,
each burden of roof to
lifts of dismal brine in
aquatinted scars, brave
drills tuning a shunned
or bouncing lunge, the
balmy night has come.

Volt pace to pale tide,
palp lip to dupe head,
fugitive colours spill
one more cold shawl

of pink, a mere strain
of the dead lift, a love
writhing, where can a
lie of its dog-star rage.

It is a crying frame, a
mortified hinge, lava
preys upon itself, the
blood bows, scent of
salt to rub along with
and behold each atom,
perfume of reason, its
skein in akeing plume.

Go, then, to the rent
look where all show
of bitter ends, crust
and rosette, simmer
and knife, throws its
face to the wall, each
skipping drift of dark
in its resting clutches.

And in the red corner,
done dusted, there to
sink, as some pillow
of rested cases, each
upon its broken foam,
the plaster gives, not
in circles of the wire
but out of our hearing.

SONGBOOK

TADPOLE MEN

Gold fish on hot beds
    so dog star rumblings
do out smooth volume
    on stones or on burns.

Now feel a cold fish
    beauty where sizzles
scar each star tissue
    of out and out skies.

Or give way, wet fish,
    for kink and clinker
to glisten while you
    earn and call it day.

So lung fish lies its
    tail across each eye
saving a moist tank
    of sheer hell for it.

As pop eyed lobe fish
    takes off with a will
so bursts its wet sac
    till quick fury gives.

And flying fish fins
      do flap so fear sent
as to skip oer mud
      is flip flop and joy.

Steer true, bony fish,
      a jaw held high for
a silk purse of egg
      so bleeds its pencil.

Or turn, hag fish, to
      look daggers on spine
in ice ink of nerves
      done to a crisp tee.

It's no use, bat fish,
      drag a sunless bulb
off each biting bell
      to dine on lost toe.

So slither, pearl fish,
      this host of hot boils
clanks on to a dusk
      now tuned to silvers.

DOUBLE YELLOW

Not for you the evening
star, nor the barbed hair

of golden stone, now as
long sleeves of the state

hold us aloft this gutter
in scarlit ways, the grit

on each blackening oath
trailing to a burn of fire.

Tooled high, our pool of
worm blaze and simmer

goes through all its stark
waltz of jam today, buds

of crimson sucked amid
the ducked stool, a swift

stitch combing the tangle
to a long imperious quiff.

When did each curl talk,
the railing rises given up

to a scarfield, so blown
to orange jets and laced

cocktails, its comfort rag
spilling a tempered lawn

where the technicians of
sensibility plough on in.

Boulder of ruffled cheek
choke your callow sash,

with clutching temper in
legions the colour of our

ribbon or lung, systems
theory with a smile, this

stain of the local to some
drum and flower of ditto.

NIGHT NIGHT

A goose bump shrinks
from high, bare places
to a stung, prone oh so

supine hem, its lounge
short of fiery loam but
tuned to fine leaves of

ouch. We're rapt, even
as a sang rind and bark
enskies the miraculous.

So off with flits to an
inkling sulk, to glitter
for a pouring crag of

scoffed milk. Unsew
such spurious sorts to
ring in sweet chunder

or snores. If and only
if turns a lip canopy on
its fetchingly high side.

No, that brags it most
which throws to wake
off this filching. You

are some clear day, as
the yoke singes into its
neck. Spoons chrome

to chamber lines, white
trash all but blown into
love oer the core sloth.

Now rends out to deck
its joy boy, he of craven
dances, skirts and crust

cuts of mister bombast
scooping up scars in the
scouring. Be our sleep

collar, be our iron hum
to none, done for by the
moon in gorgeous bone.

Well, that makes some
crime of it, or simpers
into a windy but vogue

harangue, so sparkling
to the lees. Go swift to
dull, buds that oh stills

to trimmers or breaking
bounds, that optimum
slurp clasped in a pyre.

TOME

The cage rattles, it is
        some other, quick fire
in ills, filling out pain
        strokes through whirl

and seam. I would go
        in love's blows to your
hoping deeps, so deep
        you could lose an arm

in its bindings. O sad
        earth, it still gives, it
reaps that hair scarf
        and unwraps its lips.

So shine to the wall, a
        bole of bile and broken
charm, its clearest day
        filled with rue. Where

this humid spore gives
        in open pool, there the
delights eclipse, smoke
        in me doth reign, and

now draws fire. This
        carcass is of mine, turn
sunny side up, so flush
        to this plank of sun rot.

Less said, the worse, of
        which the meanest part
and worth folds its very
        smile. Hang an upshot,

switch on to all its light
        possibilities for notes in
rogue moods. What tan
        sets a face against each

bucket of scorn, a state
        of hiding teeth, now to
flip in rock and park, o
        gags and in committee.

Something does to a
        verdant lash of chill,
to decks of colour. It
        will not suffice. You

bathe with some night
        of plate, evening spills
spread out against an
        ironed dross. Then to

break from a snug fit,
        each radiant crust, in
good tenure too, now
        to vice come file away.

Shifts in wounds, proof
        and soggy hurt where
love blurts out a horrid
        truth. It can't be taken

in, nor will this tie into
        wealth tape. You do low
in yourself, so let down
        in more flocks of talking

points, that quick and
        poor tune. It's not for
me to say. Hark, the
        antique air is smiling.

AS IT WERE

Mouth off to plunger, what farm
to little necessities glues these
   the fish to lovely, as whom food
unveils to aftermaths. On light
times untabled bulb arrays you
   come to feel its pinch, and are
of calls to sterner stuff, not one
but all told, leastwise that one
   off and folly sparkling wine bib.
But what more, what have you
to rainbow quips, slop shapes in
   late trash. No then, so thank me
furious one, done in great on fast
jibes, far from the wherewithout
   of folderol or gun romance. Make
ash bowls in this person as a cup,
teacake half best to last, no after
   you, but not to rarefy its passing
save as things fit. Do me out, my
love, in enough to be going on with.

*

One treats and coins with
the best among, how shine
is but that opened grotto

as what professes, as this
nude also takes the early
bath between the figure

of his donator and loose
of an as it were stammer
purple, lute of crater gum

*

Anyway but anyday
each and all on high
fans in no better scar

who could its novum
and normal temp on
singular ample, hip

to the nem con nods
of scary lux, cull me,
I am neither worthy

nor notwithstanding

*

And out of dominion
wake the silver string
to a lowly crime rate
and bagged flat, the

first come to, nor dare
to wield, shafts from
cloudy blandishment
to some honeyed bard

made on limpid ream
array, and is no more
master of the rolls nor
of these myriad locks

*

Yes, yes, I own as much,
   love the graceful swim
and would scatter lies
   to bring commissions in
how its tongue at least
   denies. S/he storms to
willing where a mimic
   ocean sets the terms for
lucid limbs. And who so
   bright as a transparent
gale turns the seminar to
   all soft confusion, weak
heads in pales of closer
   fold concealing, chatting
for all the dead long day.

*

In which passage
the thigh drops
from off bled

and if you do
but think it worth
can each fabulous

rise off of world
and fall confuted

*

Steady of feed bones
   as it lewdly adds
   or wings go weary

to a most ruly place
frank to last
stuck to the earth

as to its sticking place

*

Thence as to axial palms
shun the set out, a pencil
    dawn envelope, dog stall
and affiliates taken to a
steel more glitzy. Placid
is firm nearness, the licks
    of favour on of old to late
off waxen table books, the
very boudoir on slow ticks
and styles of bone in uses.

*

Off vocal grove, backwall
    leapt in steals of trip, trip,
then booted double turn of
    feet come to crash. How to
lend credence to the name
    in hand. Is there something
amid the numbers, a room
    to swing an amaretto, falls
as sweet as the hands fell
    so tuned to humming knees.

Then flits by dark kettle of
    beaten night, halls among
winces taking on themselves
    a fast toe. Sticking plasters

go under each duvet shivers,
  a freeze of primrose garden
to what long call are you
  so far from here, now it is,
seems so shorn of argument.

*

  The pile driver rings
  in late memo flasks,
  ristretto fire, in goes
  to Monday, when to

  a weak shift there's
  but a flower in your
  open look, a feeble
  task force through to

  take of day, tasto solo,
  this throng of down
  sizes jogging holdalls
  for a high water clerk

  call it a day off

*

The larkspur gives to belly
  armour, a sheen repellent,
holding their job who reels,
more for out sourcing, o yes
  if music be, nor dance shine
sweet all, nor would go tear

to lingo, near to what will
   you do me on that, sip awry
I grant, but feel its heritage,
its cloth to warm boot loads.

*

Of dish, can no quicker plum
take you fancy tied, romper
   song on bangle dance, febrile
welt and went. One suppers
with empty thickets, pays
   what compliments of hosts
as go too far on kinds. Visits
wear to this, as if to some it
   is given to matter, and not
as an idle income, their rich
scream. O what au pair for
   short shrift can ask for ease
then leave amid their cups,
can as just lit, with no issue,
   take all it is, all but trusts
flung on urchin bacchanals.

*

For only in this can assess
disease, from its good core
skill and cheater soft lob
frame serum off a fashion

what like of thine but in
brilliant landlock berths
so falls silk of the crass
to a flip flower & carpet

where its trough is filmy
repeats nothing like the
haunting in blurry flairs
as thence partakes of us

*

And in the breeze of when a
light and wonder, why does
this kindling dry, but of stale
and there without a break
so that the reach is far over
and this darkness forwards.

They hate of dull beetles, a
stubborn wheel away, such
squills to calm and in few to
reapers of the field perplex
or in the cooling wave, till
the foot of the chair bleeds.

Envy unveils its late league
tables, or brings you to your
senses, brings you to exercise
a right to buy. The postal
district thrives into a very
salivating figure, but alone
still in its malodorous barn.

*

Throw but the rub once more,
now through the melts cotton
of such even decoration, now
in pillow mantle, in trembles
for its autarky. Folds of the

scene turn much put upon, blow
darker to fine off its belated
   double star. One might say
wrong as rain, delivered for
   who in vain claims sovereign
but never attained with, you
   can but eat shoulders & load.

               *

Pleased with the found, so
        thrice earth defy'd, look to
sparklers in the brittle vent
        and yet one further thing
most pressing, come of this
        deadbody, as if some go
   for we who are only, we
        who still but sums.

FAMILIARS

I

melancholy of a style grace
hence the room only when
s/he shines a whole cloud
copy as in no. 5 above, sad

and intricate, long to tone
that quiet will to squeaky
bubble wrap or neck shine
of span grey and meal into

circles of his pictured arm
knocking stance till when
it is stranger to tights and
sunk to all affronts so tall

II

because it is die a secret
die by she breaks her wings
stills to conversing on the
done thing, come as patient

with morning of glass sky
to accented beating or sails
that ever shed to the event
of dreamy parthenogenesis

and revolting union of this
tracing ways across defiant
stones, abiding in parallel
to bring the point home

III

to its application face in a
day's fruition and folly of
jacket on to a sprung floor
not in so many words but

s/he where it gives to open
rending the slick biddable
do as can but needs pluck
and you do as you do spark

terms in the domestic open
where the bright car studies
amid the day fall against the
bark blue of feeble kinds

IV

sure blinkers of material in
bracketing out monumental
purrs appearing in the sight
and its passing of great mirth

as the plangency of its scalp
bids for inertia and affective
to the point of becoming dry
then lighting for this strange

bridge and making headway
are empty fires almost bright
but genetically fresh produce
for the jostling inch to inch

v

to be camera high, as pencil
scores but a trace in the sun
for the found texture to crow
over and do away with crews

projecting the left over pastry
place whose laughing lines to
polished glasses the tinkling
of each smile gives new parts

at least if the moon of chrome
turns to hear a way through
the usual spokes, hand held
to blend in the merging scar

vi

and the louse goes ouch to
the mother of all spiders in
from its grinding petal, so
shrewdly says the v-neck

attending to the nigh court
of the dim and loopy shake
that's noun high to stat
plumes in scart curvature

sliding down off the data
bone bind and sheer lucre
who spools their nerve tints
but stroked to fillips of pool

VII

having a mazy run whose
membrane rag glues hooves
and all the nelsons for leaf
and lifter flowing wild with

just off hundred blue whose
cut penny gem always said
come charter its glad rink
under a guild of glove plate

through the humour and
the bulb of what's suddenly
the riding harm of darkest
saffron, noise aside a grave

VIII

shoddy in shambles bundled
through the corpus snags in
loose but sweet bother and
can you hold the good frond

that heads the field so spick
and preyed upon to fevers
of leafy coral, ice and legal
balustrades in scarf wounds

whose spearing but sunny
can steel all but the urgent
places of drafty and ample
that does for the ripped aim

IX

well it beams lobe to fluff
bouquets and litter, swift
skinny ears shedding round
its sane yellow pales, thrown

light handling the white bar
through fiery bun of indoors
to span knots of parquet skirt
where did you pick that one

off to have the use and spur
her mirage, wrong foot off
tons of get you on, bubble
that glasses on to gone coo

X

physique says it all thumbs
savouring the postage nose
as loveliest peelings flood
the fun diet of camper bags

whose brass licks walk spleen
to spokes of evening downpour
the fabulous orange off zoos
to sure blue iris, now steady

and suddenly the fixed shape
sheds its stoney carriage and
suffuses a fat of late that's
quite so on a butcher's block

XI

another big hair do, quick
polls to the abominable so
enjoins s/he chimeras where
full on is no for starters

such smalls, a spruce herald
then shed destruction songs
crumb tenders for surely not
doing a stroppy rasp by the

scruff and glaze that dazzle
for which cf. the vignettes
regarding an unsightly wall
now dumb to any blind bruise

XII

the lure so inflamed and had
flinched from speed to cheap
nor for the matching towels
as our splendour clinch left

for a soubriquet loosely done
come blows of dogma to bounce
stipples that spoon our veil
and that larded hint leaving

a veritable nest of machines
in some purple tinge as would
sweep hormones into the floor
were it but a brush with art

XIII

now that's torn it, shredded
light as bowls of air space
cast that dusky scowl marked
for attention to the glaringly

obvious as to take that harsh
to task is that grown pathos
and his nibs set to pamper
even a withdrawal slip which

does our head in jumping for
the season of honey shades in
its new black, another shrug
and the floor's an old desert

XIV

but what creases till tumult
fitting rooms to hot creeds
and pants of a grand mean or
her kind eye on a steep size

and number rounding, on hold
for the focal ache of wounds
not that candid prospect to
cymbals and Venus with arms

held for swan lifts above the
package plinth, no but wonder
which gets her bust then just
browsing in its eaten frieze

XV

as while s/he gazed upward
the scruple of banter balks
its lines and veins as had
our scratch of passive good

taking a fume of subtle but
frankly wasted needle sport
that biff and boff won't do
for the coddling bruises in

also they prove our cyphers
of arrow if but hit upon by
nods as there are two things
in each revel of startling

XVI

of which not the least sand
comes some silvering of lids
shaved in wrinkles of a pull
sewn to sheds of bled balance

and daubed with bossed cuts
from sepulchral reels, where
so to lark in the short wing
call each toy our politics

of which not the shattering
but local colour, plumes in
moving pyres and the rest of
longing and a spilling clasp

XVII

some question's posed, falls
upon the bowl of the city
like aspersions, each proof
shirty and calling the table

a branch of plastic vetted
after the bees circling the
wrinkling image in teams of
oblivion, my bubbly little

hormones of darkness, and a
palpable want of carnage to
hang out with the flora and
horizons set bang to rights

XVIII

darts slip to sour as each
beholder pounces on the hem
and trails, a swelling torch
to glaze over the meadows by

what's proud but gleaned as
if a dance upon the soiled
making struck to its proper
coil, the putting on of each

tooth to gritted light'ning
come clerical palm, splash
or what have you, bar none
if hardly worth the pouring

XIX

the thing is as the staples
hand and wrung from wrists
to fill the sky with capes
and washes, like tempers to

their warranties and brawls
come grieving then carpets
show weeds, its real estate
the savage lustre swapped

for bright beads and string
to drink in cheek, a stock
of our each and several but
close to blander eruptions

XX

but as your splurge to flip
hardly does for a portable
smile cannot do but turn off
then how much for the love

of soot and scorching fills
the dirt has depth or still
beauty, well the spread took
off flush for all that daring

and a little of what does to
gloom on dolls anon or loopy
clips from point blank range
and a plunging rill of socks

XXI

so what, the kidder's at it
for the praying screen comes
to as a dishy fulminator in
all or nearly all the burns

has to hand it to you, field
of ribbed footnotes and with
quirks ironed into the very
cool of the evening then lit

by the digital whack as that
blind in war's proud ensigns
and wrinkles of this lump or
a spark but nifty once over

THE GATES OF GAZA

'What shall one born of woman be accounted before Thee? Kneaded
from the dust, his abode is the nourishment of worms. He is but
a shape, but moulded clay, and inclines towards dust. What shall
hand-moulded clay reply? What counsel shall it understand?'

Dead Sea Scrolls

'I believe that one could in principle create a normally experiencing
human being out of a piano. All one would have to do would be
to arrange a sufficient number of the piano's constituent electrons,
protons, and neutrons…'

Galen Strawson

I

its liturgical flatbed scans for
purchase so slender soul is light
toast prepressed hence to flee as

dead right remains that there's an
enormous etiquette quantity, whole
stacks on entry-level ditties, apt

yet more apt in armoured personnel
cars rusting by a separately moving
pax-brede tree, the screen driven

to token-types by imps who burst
devices for fan quality, hot stuff,
affordably top notch and brimming

and in its trivial weapon comes to
hand the jaw of dead ass, sword of
bone, a thousand foreskins falling

as flowers of Philistia till brute
force breaks its bonds, bends the
gates of Gaza, post and massy bar

to shunted bits, up stream of that
forgotten bird embost in Arabian
woods who lay erewhile a holocaust

from out its ashy womb, as eagles
spread ecliptic over predation laid
under tribute to diet coke and rock

III

altars stripped bare, honey from
lion carcasses till of raped seed
came forth a blast to answer all

so happy clappy in ecstasis, the
firebrand filing into a debugger's
whole galaxy of cloned virgin, gut

wound on its windlass, its cavity
filled to scatter blessings of salt
where metal flesh-coats explode to

let slip tortured armies leased to
light-weight image editors, abdabs
glazing round the quaking temples

IV

the cloth options out just to drop
and drag, processing straight on
back as if to a file shrunk fresco

of its miraculous trigonometry on
one stilling pleonasm, dark night
withstood, a lunch-break backslash

then simply beds down the paving
for domain values of the mandate
a wild fling through clogged rota

let fall the haughty moon to loaf
as each casual battle has a furry
idol bouncing off the windscreen

V

gild-rated, cruel sceptres break
in diaphanous properties, carrion
gripped on a steep learning curve

as birds alive feed on its number
crunch, a creaking four wheel drive
on routine patrol, itemised bills

turning to taper common offertory
elements into soft vapours, do but
scurrilities fight shy off glassy

teletype inflaming the smart new
algorithm though gut feeling says
best not leave a corpse commands

VI

apotropaic toast then cable gives
out neckerchief to sew corporases
from released minions, dumbstruck

emanations off the Heraclean down-
load stone, clubbed together, each
to their own corona, as hot whiffs

boot gutted remains off its deadly
bede-roll, drugged by reprisals as
each menu line's gone into lattice

kernels left misleadingly abstract
to spark up stonking ass, a glitch
who zooms in on the cutting targe

VII

but on for summer sun, obit rites
or hushed up industrial yarn spun
to want open source larks, a fool

of doxographical sums flickering
through chintzy scrolls set fair
for six street children massacred

before a stacked crock of vestment
bundles, icon-crackers sore tempted
down infinite regress to blue trim

while Mars gives way to the latest
Betelgeusian fancy, cache plugs in
diktats of the merest smarting dust

VIII

derided yet from slaughter free to
burn up as death squads clear the
Workers Party now no work flow

has the least string of entailment
so tight as could draw phusis off
charmingly polished pants: 'no' is

no thing's truthful constitution by
which a natural action palette is
in some sort relieved of visitation

batches, eye candy on spec popping
up attribute lists to thorny stalks
ripping through its predicate stall

IX

so necessarily vague, Job's dunghill
or sperm's yet unmatched moisture
might have led to under-the-bonnet

improvements, oh bright water font
as cosmogonical sources encode the
devotion and very essence of rubric

developed world, its mountain from
soiled naming options, cosmic fluke
or burning plagues executing a nice

touch, aide-mémoire aversion tags
sending proven icons to equivalence
till needy flies eat up the insides

X

wresting off surds on fine liquids
lets each fleeting reaper void its
quibbles, flash floods round lips

deluded play blazing fast ones off
mounted security forces, crutches
aloft, not scared to fork out for

a duff paradox of two arms lending
legend's lowest bond to let a tad
more sweet trigger in the ear corn

supplementing Grundlagen doctrines
to a tune of $300m over four years
sabres all in for invisible minima

XI

hot-swaps to worm then wing abroad
the hidden day from duels, locks in
accumulating platform-agnostic dots

of judgment, all hands to encrypted
spots, a prospect of full prisons
so satisfying to holism that ritzy

copping off takes virtual syllables,
the fancy if divisible Markov chain,
let alone justice, for smoothness of

a movie, sunk in recipes for lewd
viols or boned up flesh then waits
on the smashing party to boil over

XII

glissement heats milkiness of kind,
flight locks thirsting for atrocity
bracelets the smarting pedals deduct

as prisoned calm from torched croft,
thyrsus light to milch cow or to wit
slaughter all strangers, live pixels

inspiring sundry griefs, vile red of
sleepy meteors showering the wain in
mailed beams to blot out multi-phase

tests, micro-gloom ready for any old
ad lib protectorate before a slipshod
wine-press of the cross or pion star

XIII

but how could you stomach does bar
a silver moon from charred marrow to
odd hack daimon, engram show-trials

storming the van Neumann bottleneck
angelic spanners racing the jeunesse
dorée on surgical spirit, barbarous

mitres to kiss the pontifical neuron
on bonce swaddling: who dares sulks,
chough voice for the sump so strung

to torture any moody or pouting tyke
bidding swift remission off the much
touted itinerary of Uncle Sam's claw

XIV

crypt so cute, as for eighteen holes
in this heat, get real, ears glued
to the set, heavenly in the flaming

chariot that drags witty flesh through
the tented field to bombard the local
come what darkest succour vespertinal

may turn a remnant of noon splendour
to hear a smile through blocked rays
would the pix were defaced, a sense

of laughter quenching rood lights in
there behind its words ready to break
out in peals under some colour stooge

XV

jury-rigs squeeze in their stochastic
cooling and Turing architecture, huge
bangs bent to narrow-bands of the nude

lending a big raspberry contra idols
as if hard to identify seem blurry to
settled fuzz, entranced beyond repair

to baud beads or seem blurry at a far
remove from old soul's cosmic drizzle
the harder to blend in subordinates,

its ethical flora so vain, blunt who
do at least drop simple propositions
like flannels for a brow's even heat

XVI

out of vast tinted frames, burly pods
survey the field who cannot weep for
fresh death off some hollow jaw gone

to tear the mire of huddled trailers
light on diplomatic fallout so tender
in pandemonium, scaled blows who beat

stark melodies to rational, irascible,
concupiscible parts, and do but look
up to morning stars, nous enhanced,

lark of famine sunk on impress control
and rifled charm where the putto with
raking paw doth hale and pull its arrow

HECTOR CARP:
FRIEND AND PATRON

HIS SHELL-LIKE

Hector stalks
no kidding
a plugged ear set to cruise

the I don't think so
as it shepherds representation
along the stucco and butts

all pout and fangs
sharks set to press
the flesh and hoary dementia

so come
in the ballet
of the shadow of the fund-raiser

as the airs waters
and places turn small fry
over the mooning colon

the umpteenth intro
of spineless wonders
and sterling work

you will dance
the protestant light
fantastic and work pathos
come on all weary

FROTH OF THE FROTHER

some bosom magister
turns nasty
burns the dislike of like
into banking bruisers

medal of sad account
it seduces pulling power
to the double-breasted yawn

bloke
in gravity's graces
and clean geometries of nerve

but soft
what foam lifts yonder

mark that more and query
master killjoy on
his accursed adverbs

then a polis to chew on
the floppy pudding
and slurring

l'état c'est moi
he concurs
and changes the subject

SIGH OF THE OPPRESSED

well now Tyro
you do rare take my fancy
lend it ears
upon the bitchy flood of so so

and fallow lips
roasting pain
that each dart and stupid
gives in to

what with filmy glasses
in the prevailing
no no for once
cuts the sir custard

till no account is not gone into
but is as briefly put as this
ah: je suis miserabilist

take me to your leader
for I know his legions
have slept with his hymns to largesse

and ask only
a charm of those
who stay for the dawn

BENEFIT OF THE DOUBT

deft isn't in it
that flaming halibut
shows off the fudge implicit

lacks that pass for plot
as if to bolt
down arguments is not cool
and they don't

vengeance and charmed
give good crack
up up and away in their
racked lambs

unhand me here
ye myrmidons of obliquity
there are mortal longings
all the way up the trouser

and not a word against it
save that its
crush on the orthodox
has little to commend it

while home burns
and you slip out to the gents

MARK OF THE BEAST

slow goes the low
givings of the glib
and strangely pedestrian wildness

delegates to pain
sucking up to Cassandra
in purse and deed

more flesh to hack off the system?
and I can't say I blame you
though I do

wrongs to conceal
a true cost
as the foregoing
falls
giddy on down the gross

then takes to humanism
like a dog on praise
electric to dissolve in law

and in its light dying
what a trick vapour
and slugfest

let me slap it on
let me shiver and
smile as the broken

TREASON OF THE CLERK

famine inserts take
the stick to text
come bathos and so on

blood all over
the shop
and tyranny of the oeuvre

gone if and only
that brain in the vat piqued
to mush the purple purple

and nothing but
what instruments then
do a body lend

larks on drapes
of the piss elegant
left wondrous sensible
and not lived in

all rise for the slipper
roar of doubt and
hard noses

give me thunder
give me sky
give me sharp trousers and a lighter touch

PIANOLA

for Jo Milne

❧

trill to this   its bleeding obvious
   shifts to a spark of mellow rings
in slash funky   so stoops the oops
       upside yon sauntering logarithm
     that trots but to mortify each still
simple and bristle   such dogchat
    falls blown to log rock   the frank
but spanking fortissimo   cut now
  to one on one   dancerama done to
a lick of ooh and aah on mutinous
    pedals   pout and dimple embracing
  this   its serene and blooming kisser

*

but bear with us   signor crescendo
      bid not to quit this trifling barrow
   of darkling whim   lush dippy lippy
  stills to do lung to maths as another
 number bites the tip top mimic tusk
scissors and silence   such sparkling
 scissors   but ne'er a drought of tosh
till utilities squeak   a shunt of swish
    lurve   captain humble dancing on a
reservoir of pith   as its roux trickles
 down to tra-la-la lump   mucker zoo
    what prancing and panting s

*

stand to simper among the rancours
and wrangling city walls   a part song
and a very month o bleeding Sundays
        who as but a parchment serpent still
sheds loony toons   this bitten surface
        seeming from a quite different tooth
        a tooth takes up that speak of such
    shows boo to the fool of were   still at
large   but combs its nerve to much of
a muchness   and runs to ground on its
    tiny peels   the ends do office   that's
so so   dandy of principled allotments

                    *

lead kindly light   though loop this
        waltzing loop tricks out lycra stodge
            in stringent rules of plonking thumb
the hairy skins   shining with girl talk
        blight entailed away to boogie nights
and shed blunders   snatched from out
    now   a very bosom of shark felt levity
        each falling glory hole abounds with
fulsome bone   as its astonishing saga
    moons its fiscal falsetto   this itty bitty
    oh so gawping skip   one quota hop off
corporal elbow   deep in doggy doo-dah

                    *

her vain beam thrills   stealth bomb
    each carapace of sentiment   giving as
    good as gets   go jungle   flesh nation
        meet flint or frost disdain while indigo
    groans uncurl   the resting glaze now
of creature runs scared to miaow   biff

or purr   revenge of the killer pop tarts
        clouds of grammar shine   stammering
a dishy doll dogma   eerie bamboozling
         gone crystal hellfire   then oopsadaisy
viol of silence turn larkness risible   her
toe to quicksilver flirt   o inch of nature

                 *

sugar comes forth all the rage   dashed
     agents on each dancing shield   a flash
     of flooded loaf in sweaty logo doggerel
all hands on hoity toity   do the okey
    dokey continental   every which way to
    syrup of slop   the sight bites and savvy
shower bid to ash cake   but who gives
   a beep   team oddbod takes humdrums
to its bleating breast   and so gives of its
     cry to rectify the anomaly that goodbye
   to goodwill follows suit   their thankers
nod this way   till yes   disaster will reign

                 *

flame of rasp   some misery dunce sees
   only the do bad   the gravy wunderkind
slap happy in high blasers   give over
   spin off hodge podge and sorry purple
to leave the geezer anchored in zealous
   blots   every keen dish of our prodigious
contrapuntal largesse   now to harvests
   of cheek put to silent cheek   flim flams
rent asunder   coloratura   rise or shine
    in given pause   a throat just winging it
  in bespoke strides   a quick jiffy right off
its edge   off its full dental and rotting jest

*

hold it right there   trout mouth   no
    more zilch and star gust   nor make
        up carnage in dawn bled convictions
with an ever so   its hasty riff scents
    lay fame   flesh tone come face pâté
        a downfall dance of window fingers
each landlubber and ligger's lovepool
    wearing the scandal bra   and a most
        audacious bun for a nineteen hundred
    and ninety going on something stress
junky   criteria are go   sing lolly low
dolly go brightly   in hassle and glow

*

the shot put data boys sure do prod
    the pudding   rinky dinky triumph of
    nerd   mister kiss kiss bang bang on
salad days   and a pique-nique of ire
    one such rising goes   biff biff we are
an invincible brogue   the milky tooth
party for the dumbfounded   let rip eh?
    scions of negativity   you play but the
        coolest customer in the feeble giblets
    section   petulant lustre glammed up
in rich bitters of gimme   turn oh lilt
me in the bother   and a not so bouncy ball

THE TROJAN LIGHT

I

the Trojan light is found
wanting as cloth drapes
the page in flashes that
there is no more quarrel

with Troy nor Trojan spear
who never stole nor would
is to check these killing
seas filled in the ethic

and scudding light bands
who sue the sky for peace
as the new vague are cares
left before winter election

skeletal in a frosty train
to score no sign buckling
but a house that envy calls
and a boon in buried slips

II

ancients bussed in out of
shanty dictation as teeter
the sussed eyes bleeding a
vast camp who flows upon

each disputed slender wing
canvas spent to strip over
the live to birth ratio flak
all spruced up to fetch in

the squealing particulars
as Sabine women melisma
is blown off so niftily by
yet more perky conscripts

thrown to blue who unfurl
sheet lightning but flips
over a nuclear brolly on a
no win smile of surrender

III

wry thing and manic plumage
it's coming on all curious
and in a very real sense to
enfeeblement as crispy gloom

that's abyss for short best
of the severs yawning arctic
skin as volition withers on
that gives me fever and oh

with most audacious hand
to tongue that depends on
a media of wobbles till all
living things must die in

their immense ramifications
and seem to right here as
oxen low for the summary
execution of its posh fringe

IV

when air's dark kids come
to terrorise the hapless
all silken inner weeds do
keep such counsel to the

earth overlaid in sequins
it is that cannot strike
truce but in the shadows
sing collateral bruise so

led are progeny to rapist
valley amid sylphs who
vents then do not take a
dart from burning thighs

to the arms of a refugee
to make the plausible here
a place to park to die for
amid the azure compound

V

but first a closer look at
the day in delicate skulls
that body the giddy on a
you know how supercilious

it is as if amid top beauty
one passed a pub before
now that the fuzzy set are
on high and bubbling under

the starry throng who would
true valour see does chirp
puppy fat gods in glorious
eighty something what nots

run up encrusted in gems
for woods of the emaciated
pales and rat-nibbled hair
over a face of fresh turf

VI

the city circled by troops
pillowed softly to digest
called wings from thence
and as it were a capstone

each knitted shirt weaves
into the shroud of rubble
where the books are kept
nude so fetchingly decked

in a mascara winging each
uncut page in felt tip as
until the siege is lifted
the savage bone-cup held

square in the midriff can
quiver for the honour of
a glimmering tracer cut
through to topless towers

teeth seem bloody fine as
grey fingers of the grimace
then spoils of a gathering
shower hand cast in vain

before the onset of flicks
can sever windpipes from
the dead in no other word
but spread to purple and

not who heaped to wound
but such stunned tresses
on congeries of fertility
hence of draw strings and

surplus said to lob sharp
of nightliness all to do
now frozen in full colour
necklace and final yawns

VIII

to hides the quilted skin
hands the dangerous tain
then breakfast on screen
and made to feel the full

force of an international
community which choker
its general barely smiles
a light umbrella to feather

trigger the sentence eyes
thick on skipping page or
two what more to drift off
as luck would have it in

the window robes of such
having to have it and now
so kind of crystallising
as to feel uh-huh that's it

IX

sleek in our edible cherry
shade whence shone forth
scars spun up after hours
of grey raw on open seas

for the dazzle of its own
wrought off Apollo on no
blemish to add if nature
apart as it were its mere

of flower to open electric
curls and sewn edges are
ever swift by light divided
the jar so cold in upon to

break out in grandeur of
the glint which no amount
of furnishing could take
or put to a clouded brow

X

well a toothy scrap swims
into shame the most brief
mention of the disappeared
who no more can press but

folds dug in a burnt pocket
that aircraft have bombed
a way to the negotiating
table and a deft bathing

kind corners the surrogate
call groomed into purpose
from some ardour will suit
the matinee nymph in sore

digits that lavish somehow
till a cost of which upshot
is human terms and open
to views from Machupicchu

XI

just as a door policy sheds
its loose cannon and party
machine should its stubble
disaster strike made more

so over the grey pastiche
where opposition flowers
to duck out on the resort
charge of even-handedness

forthwith as a most sweet
and selfish gene laying in
siege to turn to personal
effect that the assembling

phalanx head to ship light
in holds for spiked arrow
takes the plough on a ride
of squalor passing rampant

XII

so is it any wonder before
the people's front to top
bear all cut to the bias
in a slick but nervy scarf

then shadow box but in the
last quarter cannot evince
the requisite transparency
ditch of dailies churning

stuff their own campesinos
heed as damp hands clutch
the rip sheen now demanded
of each shark passport and

are given the bird to drag
the foot when all around do
pale and pale shadows of a
former plant patent in fist

XIII

so to comb scolds vulgarity
its closing teeth not quite
as it ever was how clients
halting in the knife halted

yawn frankly at a neglect
done for some proxy theatre
run up upon the still clasp
and far conflagration whose

breach of all for which our
warmest hand is played out
on the dark plinth and rude
Europa stood now smarting

the rape the blood in pelts
how rapt stings torn from
its holding spine so much
as spent their brink thing

XIV

then slag heaps and trim
half cut into white amble
can steam the pretty shit
for whatever else is going

with the dump on a porch
still gowned to trains and
shrouded with rosy-fingers
of the usual dioxide would

you but bustle along in the
prime and closing of a calf
done to flavour the low cut
who skims the light dying

cocooned in ruche quivers
now birds will unfold them
that flighty arch as Nestor
does but suddenly drop off

XV

the ideal of the hourglass
weighs yet more in swirls
for the gods of low-hanging
the like of which has been

spread as pencil mutton
over such plush footage
all up with it as in hoops
turn mobile to score thirst

as the censor gives a blind
well hullo there and needle
for some sea breeze taking
the brow found and dead

that their silky remnant is
said to hold a scar's digest
due to a lack of low flame
now broken and to marble

XVI

as shrines go it's exposed
for sure in its stale gravitas
that it is so nearly overdone
but not enough to fill in the

ash pits now inwardly grim
with the radiance and furry
volk epic but you know the
stiff terrains of their 'time'

the growth left to grind out
crusts who bleed the fresco
then turn to beg a rural set
while the return of privation

stalks the people's saloon
in nearly new retail gothic
well known in each manner
and shorn from its benefit

XVII

not to mention if in passing
there is much to preserve
amid the frisky cheek that
crops the up and coming

and works over a foot stool
beat to a smoking gun and
a stalk close to fissures and
landslides seeping into faces

hedged about with a model
smirk set to daze or mop up
the fossils and as if that were
not enough its spent quality

so fried to an empiric that
prattle rains on to tease out
plunging lines and umpteen
bows tied onto the carcass

XVIII

so much for natural history
and the fast price crumbles
as each string of canc'rous
light reserves a sentence for

calm valued in sacks on the
dock and said to rough house
the bleeder of sleepy screeds
pushing out the shifter prop

that spells a shard of bone
as parts heed off the smalls
then standing units spawn
ancient scaffolds and gulp

or tune into the spun wind
sparking off the petrol heads
and a sable track unfurling
its fast and savvy corruption

XIX

not for translucent skins
stacked up on cornflakes
can shift each bluish viol
even when said to look the

part as in intimations of
the emaciation upon all
of the dancing part lights
almost burnt and in fall

the curtains fled up stairs
shuning its property guide
and the golden Sheba look
stuck upon our soft water

where it nearly came to a
war for frayed nerves that
are best left to the sinking
but seamless prose of fur

XX

parting as the cloud swallow
each shocker and judicious
toppling ankle spread down
before hurling abrupt stock

still plenty seen and stood
mounting the cream chords
off each bit of cordon-bleu
would but the truce stench

stitch craquelure for booty
scuttling the first sky blow
in somewhat feral wandering
to carry out of the mouths

of stern child and faction
come forth shoot blue and a
rendered dawn is yet evening
scrawls under house arrest

HOMAGE TO MAYAKOVSKY

❋

SIX ONE-WORD POLITICAL
HOMEOPATHY POEMS

THE VOICE OF HIM THAT CRIETH IN THE WILDERNESS

isms

O YE MAD COWS OF HINDSIGHT

wasms

THE POUND AGAINST A BASKET OF OTHER CURRENCIES

karaoke

ALL THAT IS SOLID MELTS INTO SMOG

propaganda

TO EACH ACCORDING TO THEIR NEEDS

prescriptions

A SOUNDBITE BEATING ABOUT THE BUSH

freedom

amid the glamour of the secular and frankly godless hall
it falls to song to shimmy on down and sing it like it is
or would be if the law of speech acts did not beg the question
what ought or is can tether art to the greater promise of love
in short, where's Bacchus when you need him now that Pan
is just the god of silly sheep and savage earth can splash
the hour in flowers till the sheep come home without letting
slip more than a kiss of lasting bonhomie and not that
open song where love tramples on the slippery powers
of church, rite and the Levi-Strauss memorial kinship shuffle

but come now, savage earth, dazzle the patriarchal sky
so open love can saunter through each warring thought
and furnish room where two can live as one, if not quite
united then dodecaphonic in their radical harmonies
you see, we're short of tone rows that don't sound anxious
now that rime's gone the way of the dog collar and there's
more than a splash of cringe in words like bride and groom
and that old plot which equates husbands with farmers

I think it was Hector Rottweiler who thought marriage
might be the last chance saloon in which to shape bonds
against the prevailing hymn-sheets of inhumanity
but there's a whiff of dogmatic hair-shirt under that collar
as if Proust had the last word on prisoners of desire
when you and I know that true love means never having
to say whose turn is it to do the washing up? or blow me
if freedom isn't the conscious recognition of necessity
which reminds me, now that Marx has replaced God
as the author of the Holy Family, it was Karl who
claimed that this relation lets us grasp how far
human nature has become, well, human nature, has
reached, that is, its most individual, most social being

this is hardly the song with which to practice duets
of private bliss, but if freedom as marriage can
only become general with the abolition of capitalism
it just goes to show that the dodecaphonic tone row
is no bed of roses, as we hope for roses over Mill Road

in the wish for more reciprocity than just giving gives
it's a comfort to be told that the planned economy
lives on now that Habitat has a centralised list:
may you be showered in soft furnishings when potlach
is but a wink in the eye of fiscal probity and may sun
clear a path through those clouds of ideology in which
RAE plus TQA equals SFA: no, we wish you better,
more human things than are dreamt of in that philosophy

call me a young Hegelian, but there's spirit in the
making when one plus one is more than two, a family
of more than bright ideas, as efforts to be in another
come to a chorus of recognitions too subtle for others
to more than wonder at, and it is wonderful, as we gaze
into the future, see you happy and hope it's a sign
that we'll be happy too, happier still if we can share
in your joys long after the moon's made of honey

TROUBADOUR UNBOUND
on his belated inauguration

Pound et toi, mon ami, mon
hypocrite professeur, camarade
de poésie, now here's a wonder
done out of the chilled section
best left to irrigate the parched
stones of the Orange Room, here's

to the return of the silver hounds
oh roll over there Swinburne
so indiscrete when numerous
when the bottle bank's hungry
and many a dog-eared index
card gathers rust in the greying
vaults of research fitness clubs
where the latter-day Thoreau
might take a leaf out of death
and profess himself more than
a little pleased by a hard day's
slog on the word-processor,
no, not now and not for us
there's more in them thar Cantos
than is dreamt of in TQA
and however you shuffle that
forcefield which repels as often
as it attracts, the thing is
you're a guide in the valley
of the one-eyed pro and just
so economical with the truth
that bruises can be so purple
and though poetry's a mug's
game with nothing in it, we're
in it together, come crime
and carping critics, however
the much vaunted nursery waltz
of usury and Medici gold
might be really spoiling us now
we'll leave the church-spotting
to the Renaissance blokes
and turn once more to song

THE PRINCE OF BAD AIR
a.k.a. the man from C.C.C.P.

come zipper codes
    come date the shade
the mooning round wine-rucks
each sylph in sandals
as his silver streak machine
        sups on bloke soup
staggered through

to bullet points

pints   as solid phantasm
of corn   but ye dogs
  of cupidity   woof
am dozy libidinal
           let's slip
one over the bar sign

beaming from armpit to armpit
yawns to grace leisure
swinging bosom in negligee
distray a cheese dreamer
      in his dogged   schmooze
vultures round her bloom
        whose fade to rotundity
leaves the woolf to pale
  in the pink   going puce to floral

AMIS COMME COCHONS

knees brush as the crack is of
enlightenment and of some
interminable digression the like
of which betokens majesty

as when the theory boys
come marching in on ice
hipster that's slack dialectic
with a gift for high darkness

her amplitude as canvas for
our minor embrocation through
seams soft as clouds of putti
so rub the denim engines but

cannot bear too much hippy
ham fabric rips till on the t-shirt
AMOR VINCIT OMNIA calmly plunges
into your still attending jaws

SEASONAL GREETINGS

another December morning does alarm time
stonily advancing towards boot camp hilarity
with the DJs, and what if several mornings
could stretch out south and fly the week
a flock of buses all at once taking the easy
way out along the trans-Europe express
while you, me and assorted vultures prey
on scripts like the falling of the weekend

into someone else's arms, someone else's
pocket. Xmas is coming, relenting cheers,
Xmas is coming, well did it ever leave the
cupboard stuffed for the eternal return and
no we don't recall the siege of Leningrad
save in the most pressing of food queues
while the DJ cranks up the contempt bass.
There's no ice on the inside, which is good
only a tickle from central heating to meet
the chorus of mobiles and sheets smiling
somewhere there's a contract out on you

CUT TO THE QUICK

who as it were in the very pink
can saunter above petty cash
in yet another faultless expo

come spills to greet the guests
so warmly, with such obliquity
that will do for me till day's end

and later, fresh from the news
of a quite previous masquerade
the crooked elbow has its say

taken to number off like some
sweetner held to corrupt the
sweetest teeth among staples

but off! off! ye floral chemise
let fly in your pacific loafers
such stark and soapless arias

that get up on the brush off
out of shapely dancing as we
who are about to lie salute you

100 DAYS OF MAMMON

he walks, he talks and then
some, and there is murder
in his eyes where once a wind-
capped orator flew off a shiny

plate of still to be assembled
loves and sang of old the killer
sound-bite so chuffed on song
going boom boom so few uhms

per drift it's the way you tell
them disappointments to keep
like how you fell in with lamé
slipper crews on route to slicks

or gems re the half-wept stare
that's so broke why fix me up
et le rat a mangé le biftèque
who holds the fort as a beau

cirque du monde and nature's
a destructive principal that's
a fact cue extensive laughter
leaving beasts for badinage

and the zoo's so you it drains
slackers of public calamity
now some Chambre de Justice
holding out for singular revels

each to fuck an epistemological
squirm for a game of soldiers
done real low maintenance
that the nature of the gauze

is its purpose here today and
gone to Jerusalem flag happy
well in a sense I grant you
a kind of slide-show of Being

with woof woof in the lock-up
or bad flava so idolators are
topsy huh? weapons of choice
done calm and final warning

up to the task and even if I
too have insisted that there's
an idiocy to evil it's a spirit
of malice to make such specs

oh pants they boom to curl
up for spanking fine maths
and long primitive additions
hear how with cross'd thumbs

they play ave mum whose box
is flicker still for a back drop
ah me how does our grog go
will bloomer into such folds

to avoid the barking prizes
and a hint of spring wafters
a right shed-load of morals
what less could you wonder

nor I, not even attachments
yet more 3-d images, yawn
so still the water gently seeps
as if www.Noah.com's come

among us bearing glitterati
ooooh, the flatter the better
says yonder Monsieur Luddite
it is the though that counts

indeed much appreciated
and the same to you, though
I say go! go! go! Mister 2000
and your many damp patches

come waltz said liberal circles
we're off to Barcelona to catch
a hint of '36 that still lingers
in the air amid the stench of

urban regeneration a.k.a.
kapitalismus the euro-way
then mice are lightly bored
but perhaps there'll be room

for another moody lunch when
the new year is not so new
though even in Derry there's a
franchise opportunity culled

from exalted necklaces of cloud
gone fable and fable that no's
not among the massing ranks
nor can be headed, never fear

all in for bonbon delicatessen
naked agronomists in Russian
for business so hot to forever
defuse the situationist in you

c/o the other of all song with
this ghostly incisor in its flesh
syllable now you see it plain
to bury alive the flaming neon

bombarded to a picture skip
as if stars are acrid fools set
in whose wonder buck naked
sky this but turns to carry in

say-so or falls in with a moving
regime when you do 'human'
they take you for a humanist
of the sheepskin persuasion

larks from the razzle up low
who can't see for speakable
joys so strange in darks to say
nothing of your blistered looks

SMOOCH-PUNK FUSION

sunk riff contra payola
it's a family affair now
Exmouth market calls
at the top of our dials

or going on something
over daring funk drole
fringes so stirring still
amid the balding lyres

take that you freebird
that dash of daft quiff
left to mingle with the
newest pringle jerseys

spangled chevron turn
to rusty jacket braces
set to the continental
dorf disco bus or angst

trims the strummer's
paw flaying those air
chords on dog drums
for the plastic chicken

so how you fought the
law and won a cheese
grin that tunes smile
riots in the key of life

OSTRICH TAKES OFF

flocked machines curl up on roughage
and run up tacitly the extreme savvy

felt to rumble and as the earth burns
what just in does off on cattle & horse

now ostrich flesh has the driving seat
right in there on joined-up burgerism

what convertible bond do savour each
I mean puh-leese if the *vice Américain*

is so becoming then the *Sprecher* can
take the first hike among said equals

let the mission steaks go fuckabout
or more sooth on horde or lard lounge

run to blunt risk glades as you were
and wouldn't it be nice to stay clear

if not tight to the pterodactyl wind
plucky in pink among roasting birds

now summer's here and up in flames

HOMAGE TO MAYAKOVSKY

Philologists,
            cyber-snouters, ye olde
                        shit-stirrers!
from ordure and the tacky night
            deadlines are come again
                        like agit-pop
that may tip
            your tongue to
                        one more 'heugh, spit.
What more
            will our cognitive codgers find
                        for papers
      to tut the curious
                        thaws,
that are – well,
            hard boiling, tinctures of pulp
                        those fluffy pups
                              or friends who paste the heat.
Right then,
            off with your fancy optic, prof bloke,
                  take a turn on categorical
                              intuitions
                        and why not, so unlikely –
moi,
            foot and mouth butcher
                        now pump primer
finds the call-up,
            nay sanctioned for lost elections,
                        freezing on the edge
of drooling pastures
            where the silver spoon mobs
                        are hot for more silver.

Not so, Aurora
       (her, the no-logo whore),
              old cradle snatcher
  of many a maiden pamphlet
               and worse
umbrage,
    fivers,
           datcyls for line dancers
morning puke and the dawn choir
               quelle horreur!
Our savage bird-fancier
       does his cheeky cataloguing –
he'll check out each sweet digit
      tout suite,
          you mark my scars
now feathering the flames
       lest the anthological beasts
         refine harm
  into fist-flights of a sorrier syntax.
But what's to do?
      amid power plants humming
         the seven veils of democracy,
    what savour to pare?
         or cull to carp among
our software
    vacuum packed herbs
       city heights and private skies
         the social on sale
  like lost leaders and a co-op funeral.
Moi aussi –
    running the messages
       leaves chowder
  where the critique of slick taste
     browns and foxes at the edges.

Lighten up!
    comrades of the posthumous,
        here's another quiver
            felt-tipped quipster
        showering the poetaster anon.
We'll crash the lank
        and second-hand songsters
            as quick for it
as any lunging theorist –
        we'll come unto you
            unAmerican activities
not like the mission statements
                or retro Celanians
    who know the local, but too well!
        our whispers will tickle you
                over pain and schism,
            over quiffs of choirs
                    and committees.
The ruins will mumble on
            with a not-so-Tintern sparkle
    (con gaz)
        but with the lippy
            in Cupid's lyric dash,
not like the footnotes
            under the curator's fondle,
        nor with the reviewer's
                belated charms.
These damaged goods
        will find their way
            among remaindered pyres
    and lucid,
        risible,
            irrepressible,
                share a pillow with you

as are with us still
                    the public spas
                              etched in lime facades
                                        so shaded with acid.
These snatched
                    of fossil songs
                              join the lost pines
and are cut out for
          pronounced ire
                    contra 'National Trust',
so livid with alienated labour
                              and slips of death dues
                    that each flat moth
                              lost to itself in electricity
will flame
          and then combust
                    in the halo of obscenity.
Et voila –
          in party togs our nouns undress
      and skip through
                    the prosodic scandals
                              on tender toes.
There shift the nibbles,
                    grim with e-numbers
          for sacrificial finishes,
                    thermal loads ascending –
                              and to attention.
Pint-glass to pint-glass
                    heaving over belted horizons
the heavy dudes
                    arrange
                              their deadly extended sequences
      with an epigraph too far
                    seeping from each side-pocket
and the much-loved
          arsenal of lathed put-downs

                                        saved for the bar exercise
                        of critical snap
            chop to the knees on the qui vivre
                                    to explore the wounds
        with puns and quips
                            and all the fire that envy breathes.
And all this army
                        armed to the false teeth
            with years of weasel blinks
                                to their eternal credit
and then assembled
                        for some thumping majority:
        we throw it around, then away
                                the civic globe and co.
Tribune
            of the slumbering proletariat
                            (who s/he?)
    that's ours all over
                    scorned,
                            mourned,
                                    bosomy too.
All are called
            under the troubled
                            down years of realisation,
    we've done the Gesammelte Schrifte,
                                like you do,
        as an analysis of fridge remains
                        to dance over each best-before,
and even without shelves
                        we could aver
                with whom to muster,
                                a side to call our own.
But negativity
            came of its own
                        not out of Adorno's hat.

Over dinner and afters
              what whistles among our robes
when memos set managers to howl
       the very howl
              come harlot's cry
                     that ran down office walls.
Let that bitch Cereberus
       show his teeth
              to Hektor Rottweiler
so stirs the
       same again,
              and one for yourself?
Die,
   die, my text,
              like any temp or co-worker
left for dead
       amid the station-wagons
              of the photocopier.
Sweet nothing
              we give
       to boast 'exegi monumentum' – pah!
sweet nothing
              for pebble-dash cladding
                     for gold leaf on the spine!
We're in this species together
                     let's get it on
   out of shambles
              into the liberties
                     and lay down the ruins
  of our social being
              a.k.a. the long hike to socialism.
Philologists,
       fasten your lexical life-belts,
  we're headed for a bumpy ride
              down the glassy surge,
                     when recherché items

such as 'arbitrage'
                    'drug tsar'
                            or 'serotonin'
            swim as filaments of tumbleweed
            hushed into the nuclear winter
                                        of our fathers –
                how green do the valleys become!
For you
            of iron lung and buns of brass
        who's left?
                            but those licking their wounds
                                    those taking turns
                    on this treadmill
                            or the kit that walks.
So through a train of tears,
                    we're half way to popsicles
                            ice-men
            our fossil songs
                    left for slurry and screed.
Come,
        universal songsters,
                            let's step up on the quick foot
                down the long stairwell
                                    to the end of days.
There's hardly a note
                    left in the drawer
                            barely a floppy
        or rich-text format
                            sculpted for perishing
and, to be frank,
                mes amis
                            the undercarriage may fail.
That said, I'll swap you glory
                                    for the sustain pedal
called on
            by the Friends of St. Just

                    our crimson-headed dancer,
out beyond the thumping throng
                    and those fellow-travellers
                              of Trot and Gentry,
but we'll stay up eh?
                              like flexible friends turning
leaves of conversation
                    from each to each
                              going one better than the night.

[SIC]

metallic tongue shivering
on for the wreathing year
so tall flops off how yes
turns night gales to nose
on costly string and lyre
for exultant mistress bee
who readies the scorpions
and so say 'raw' material

on the line 'good' nature
your pretty eyes away far
it's lonely knee up ahead
when to gentleman styling
who gives a shimmy and on
come strip the xmas scree
eg. kermes, cochineal and
dye derived from pickling

the irk of whose roots go
yield to great permanence
and the flame colour took
up easy peskiness for fun
run sicamour in cypresses
imperishable as flummox'd
that's putting it sweetly
to open the surgical acid

would o would on a hiding
quite meaning well but so
eccentric he could be our
virgin of department song
I just said her thing for
authorities sang piss off
to viols the calling sark
just into shorts that eel

of autumn on the raw neck
with purls or finger loop
in lieu of fallibilist to
reserve loss frenzy shock
fitted up right and girly
so that 'proper' does for
short work of an absolute
the schematism to fade in

we loved all things about
her especially the finale
tamping down off droplets
in zone to urban savannah
that hung corse whose eye
renews the wintering scar
it would but bruises glow
to run and mock the gloom

and the flying fuck's now
seen to lips and learning
carbolic in the start huh
setting all at naught new
my shoe rose and sore pip
for the tawdry takings or
what lasting sterility to
set jelly edicts to dishy

rack skint in shit furor
running for a priori top
stunning lack of politic
in the singular want gut
shell shacks in its minor
gruntest thou shimmering
for the bald ceiling and
evening's sewer bleeding

return to previous cream
in the fold closer scale
to skeleton army in this
night exotic half the ah
showing the during skein
timbre is as ramp breeze
lit to beat the pulp dog
calling on patriarch wit

and at the border mouths
each drawn vulcan patter
into the duck duck cower
fickle sauce held out to
faith for all the yellow
who shoulder the bathing
and each slight held for
the beauty as in leather

that's send for a blague
to fill in for furnishes
where escarpments cut in
deepest darkest lie here
by my side of cramp calm
and then take up to lift
fanning out fang goodies
drawn for one night only

rack visible then friend
and rails used for blunt
unto edge viz. man [sic]
is free and his will can
take the claim for class
into its fantasy leagues
to bland radical evil as
mysteries take for crops

by attempts than augment
happiness whilst barking
up their opposing torque
half and hard perfecting
who show the way to ripe
as in the romantic bodes
to be done well to other
and rare to mean radical

all our judgments blousy
bled to standing collars
the scarf worn to lights
and the potential wedded
to gadding about town or
stir but patience huddle
make your own colloquial
will can to flaming arse

the log does fitter duty
as to brunch parting eg.
more on the hoof for the
hog standard demos sinks
who rooms to the sploosh
with his paw munificence
in hurt suppers then put
down for mires on stucco

hand to hand the shocker
and cheating stock pales
before the up and coming
years he blew in promise
and another scare tactic
the film noir pragmatism
withering on pain coming
up like its notable curl

SWEEPING NEW MEASURES

ꝑ

1

hot foot to it finest of fine bit dead,
as they thought, the rash crinkle fires
when lax on scars they open in paraffin

and heads fell, shame each lost penalty
who takes up to run such as idiot booze
prevails the want or pupil lux too true

will you no take the bitters sonny dog?
and shoulder the vanity, shoulder frown
for each wee bit fire, dead for gristle

2

till rid of light, the mountain rebound
grows treachery, nothing too grand mind
you and your mockery of the kitchenette

save succour and twin all flouncing on
stocking cloth taking its exception and
dim the dimmer, our very own ooh or aah

no pick one of the fit cloth finishings
spent on threads, bedside lexicons or a
fading fancy for the darker gong on oil

3

is there no ripeness to her put me down
would tuck the slanging deuce upon each
little advantage in the flattery raffle

well all sorts, yes taken, or kept back
spank to loafer now bounces dawn to fly
show me that rise and I'll squander all

now hail the savage sparrows holding up
Venus to general motors as Vulcan ticks
set to worry the sheep grazing in maths

4

while the truth-seeking pump going like
a clap slips down upon its knees to beg
to differ for 'modern' read 'human' for

swarming blazers yonder door for 'logo'
read 'logos' something for it sprinkler
and spring oral chorus grand for 'test'

read 'text' that's right vital burdened
with a wondrous palm upon the morrow to
flip on the least cry's fumbling morass

5

hand, hard, not to mention vile in show
that goose du jour squeaking go on like
crème wasn't built in a toast, falls in

and her zip code said Beirut first drop
then check lark with the stripe pyjamas
spent en route to the Peshawar corridor

as spectacles of the best the aid could
subvent, may I proffer you another lick
as that done wing scumbled c/o Philomel

6

therefore, how drole, what's so precise
more even than a 'surgical' strike thus
the bladdered dead sea for weekend blah

like you knew the personal plunder trip
was just a sap way of currying desserts
ferrying up tough-luck supper scenarios

one after another how we laughed, smelt
the coffee and dreamt in body liners of
sandbags at dawn, tides turning to beer

7

then the caprice takes an unlovely side
for a bell-weather postulate, dead right
being without data along a heart string

vibrant, perm said to blow away the web
in its live-in plug, day's spent wonder
blended to hours upon relay, more crash

and darkest crumble our social services
in blood clots, plans to frisk even the
ballet fan rattling a cage marked Weber

gripped by the mood and light pollution
by listing then a little bit barking or
shift dresses fitted and flaring all as

the demure set to expose more loopholes
in the palest latin of tracer fire then
ardent dusk slips hints at a late final

sweet nothing cradled for the love shot
go easy as fear encrusts the longer sky
and merest thunder comes as a trembling

9

up to the integer bold of works dancing
to have some equivalence in Aristotle's
catalogue on the boo which was intended

what stop, use or efficient cause to do
some grist of the classical goal-posts on
the move playing location upon location

and men do alter at the birdland spills
from the UK negative territory to speak
then delete 'of them' before passing on

10

mutter mutter re economic impact downer
did I hear mispoke by your minus growth
called like we see it to a frail breeze

at the same blind there's that stimulus
related to, and an aid to, stunners all
contra strident's strict flutter (yawn)

still, the mood has changed, portfolios
fissure into belly up tickled to a pink
and bacon rind, where the sheen is prim

11

on the counter-cyclical play so to puff
clean up, showers of vibe as by crucial
you mean they are consuming confidences

set to serve the transcendental withers
blown around as hair days take the turn
for the ethos that most pampers the low

just a lard sump longing for a blessing
not that you take the fly blown platter
a.k.a. a new week off from t.v. dinners

12

but that could prove a false smile, all
this as winter approaches, what refugee
can bear the scoundrel and shabby queue

hail to thee, ye bang to rights blinded
for a world food pivot making us a rift
as the topos shows up to remainder moi?

of course this does not save the bruise
while the phrase 'classical' passengers
takes a sharp intake of blonde romances

13

and skinny fries with everything, totty
that holds sway before the unhistorical
do much as the tightly knit express ire

then principle surely triples antiquity
application pending, meanwhile upon the
village classroom silence falls for the

communiqué rumoured as intense pressure
would deflate all the learning left for
what they call a closed military buffer

14

what fag packs in the bland and bulging
which are, limply, machines for a choir
whose yardstick is flung as a bee-sting

floating upon cycles of violence dulled
according to a cloud that does but seem
too lively when it's a gag on the cards

and when is it not, spilt brine barking
in the shudder, stank, sole to shingles
is that a place so simply left for home

ECK'S COLUMN

for Alec Finlay

They Lees
An Axe Inexorable
An Oxymoron
Pie Thanksarus
Gorgeous
Palm Any Tease
Sock Rat Ease
Play Dough
Harris Dawdle
Duh Mock Rid Us
Yew Clipped
Epic Treatise
Sissy Row
Lou Grease Us
Jay Zeus
Org.us Tyne
Plot Minus
Pro Tack Walrus
Bow Easiest
Heavy Sinner
And Some
Abbey Lard
Ach Wine Us
Dumb Scrotum
Will Yum Hokum
Don Us Mower
Air Asthmas
Mont Aim
Copper Knickers

France Is Baking
Deck Art
Plays Ask Al
Lime Knits
Spin Hoser
Domus Hops
Toilet Lock
Eye Sack New Tongue
Park Lee
Shafts Furry
Bum Guarding
Did Her Owe
Rue So
Day Fit Whom
Eye Can't
Fished Her
Freed Rich Shell Ink
Hay Gull
Shopping Hour
Calm Arks
Freed Rich Angels
Queer Que Guard
Freed Rich Neat Char
Whose Earl
Smarting High Digger
Bird and Truss All
Which Gin's Time
Lou Cash
Fay Burr
Bench Ah Mean
Ah Door No
Mark Who Sir
Jump Alls Arch
See Mont Both Were
Myrrh Low Bounty
Hammer Our End

Jack La Con
Al Too Sayer
Mash Hooray
Me Shelf Hook All
Have Her Mass
Chap Daring Da
Eleven Us
France Van On
Nigh Home Jump Sky
Sol Crib Key
Stand Lee Car Fell
Shield A Loose
Chilly And Grows
Beer Bored You
Chewed If But Fleur
She Cheque

GO FIGURE

'Solon used to say that men who surrounded tyrants
were like the pebbles used in calculations.'
Diogenes Laertius

'When shall we have men of a universal spirit?'
Oliver Cromwell

'Without him Caesar would have stood alone...
He's the universal soldier and he really is to blame...'
Buffy Sainte-Marie

'I have never reached the true centre,
where art is pure politics.'
Tom Raworth

For every blemish of determinate song
come fallen drifts upon untold bitters
and shall be some equal and opposing
with the infinite sadness of families
carrying the dead by them so lightly

here a fear, there a broken down promise
as if some law of excluded middles
disproves the early bucket of the just
and callous digits ill at these numbers
now fall breaking in upon hostage news

*

This imperium's eagle spreads ancient wings
as the saying goes ahem friends Romans
and globalists most dextrous ego-surfers
of the remotest control say go figure
let slip the bristling clusters and gas
from each harsh Doric column stabbed long
and hard into a ruin of sea and dimpled air
most cleaving indifference over physical
features that depict no political borders
all the solids gone the way of amalgam
lost upon spicy chicken wings as claws
do special resolutions in pink cartoons
nails down tankers the chalk on board thing
and the gas is all for oil, galley slave
of this grade class fellow-guzzling petrol
and not to bury Caesar or mock his father
but stacks of cheap beer waiting to party
till even a spangle-toed smoke akimbo
can't fully wipe the thought of a pretzel
turned t.v. assassin exploding Cubans
spread far across the axis of nonsense
a.k.a. the death squads of those with most
squeezing the life out of those with nothing
the words bang to hearts turning real hard
so scream now or forever hold up paws
for the cut chaser doing that's all folks
still counting on meltdowns to explosion
on the ghosted spread-sheets of Halifax
the embrace as plausible as a love train
of leaf-peepers off to blushing Vermont
so much chasing after reddening glory
and the little matter of chemical yarns

*

Onward to the contrary it is
        syntax troop motions
standing orders in a phalanx
        tipping the remainders
and small lips calling revenge
        be prim with the primer
come distant and knitted brows
        then autumn folds take
to scupper the jokingly warped
        azure scale of the trait
but hardly illumined by same
        faked to a sad choker
with a grammar of solidarity
        under an aegis of nouns
bled to stable bit and foam and
        then sacrificed, frankly
further to the up and coming
        for which thorny witness
read in the obvious fresh aura
        such that flushing roots
spread their exponential terror
        right up on schematism
and each interrogative chamber
        scrubbed and sleeping
among good but tortured doves

*

Sort codes move on slaying in costive eyes
thou stock and spool thinned out to drapery

and well shook tracings in name or crumble
while a saving trace is put down to salt

how over much as much that wanton draws
parchment turns on carbon till pages fray

hardly raging as they lay claim to fields
then spreads for the pulp of leaving parties

down through nibbles and a short trivium
chipped and spun to gossip, food and t.v.

*

Swiftly on the hook of x
the opponent of the latter
falls just as opus grudges
crack up fractions of day

cast off and left for knives
as in plaster or patter fire
no tomorrow and coming
so soon comes to nought

blonde or gone as around
it pleases all the sack log
and still plangent parade
as the call to an executed

summary not what least
throws beauty off the tick
tongue to wag ooh so not
and come off it says next

*

How so ever but through equilibrium
lost then turned to a fabulous scalpel

where the converse applies to the ratio
for instance a callous rocked to edges

or feed tending to scale up calmer ties
so wrapped around an attention scaffold

that to you is gurgle and burnt hotpants
a beach of bruised pleasure going too far

beyond pavilions and the setting rain
who is not ground out nor come together

*

What bias fixed
or how passed
in liquid aether

thy coop active
lo wise lobe or
obsequious orb

among ministers
and right weary
fair image of the

flood of bounty
said the ferment
said ruined deep

*

After   ether   pitch   packets
      skipping   who   stiffs   our
deftest   finger   that   tantara
    mildly   period   niche   eek-eek
sunk   through   lived-in   stroke
     as   for   swishest   things
flung   dribbles   then   swill
    then   mmm   pout   liner
cushions   the   whirling   streak
    party   beast   peaking   peaked
oh   just   meringue   dusted
    for   dazzle   dubbed   poppy
now   doing   what   stalks
    porosity   from   bends   proper
shouting   glory   glory   blunder

*

Drawn till infinites stale
then hideous light crawls
off gracile to sloth touch
no pearl but larded fives

whereas once sung brine
falls in a speeding crust
showing napkin economy
and nothing to finger but

two eggs plus four toasts
triangles to buttery mush
snare slider off to flounce
mumbling the lash saucer

sunk without volte plaque
where the focus for firing
goes starkers for the call
tuned to a foaming ellipse

*

Sing death to parallelism
sir spiked colon chirping
flock mannerisms flexed
to harping gruel or such

such arrogation fiddling
over the grinding poor
a hymn to the prevailing
batteries spent on tributes

for the crested screamers
the unsighted basilisques
shaking each turret scoop
called to the mine fields

next stop Damascus

*

After Jenin what song of
songs seeps still through
the scrip and pearl till
dark breath fills on lung

and first is as a fist gone
to what dune it grounds
yet to die for in garlands
among smarts and staves

but one more cypress tiara
spelt down a wig or two
would what water and melon
bleed on in a strange land

before laying down to sleep
among ancient diseases
hawks upon willows who
cannot lay themselves to rest

*

Put to pieces and spark in the window
gone all pointilliste over stress pixels

the bundle upon bundle shifting noises
and the example given makes a pity

for the slight slipped in as a placeholder
among streamers turning that pink curtain

where the *it* so held shows up property
and there's a sign saying mended blazing

equals haze and fenced with fenestrations
over much that scolds but never comes last

*

The   practice   purrs   along   smudge
     sake   where   but   ladders   lift
then   the   lean-to   giving   curves
     takes   to   turning   light   angles
showing   white   above   the   ankle
     shimmer   upon   arches   in   graphite
whose   regular   squeeze   lends   room
     and   figures   without   lawns   or
measure   upon   axes   in   furs
     turns   and   turns   about   consoling
the   joy   of   nihil   bowling
     path   pursed   soul   of   dance
slightly   off   centre   then   leaning
     right   through   the   shift   exacted
winged   in   the   heart   spark
     whose   burnt   middle   shifts   break
and   trace   each   largesse   looming
     not   much   allowed   paper   stacks
that's   not   quite   not   chance
     whose   fresh   stone   done   prime
and   got   even   what   larks
     shifted   in   gravel   and   fountains
strung   out   laces   come   gracing
     in   the   mean   and   ground
into   its   make   shift   marks

*

Rank for a remedy
less rigid and more
part of the rounded
muscle or soupçon

rounding up option
swabs to a near ruin
does personal airing
but less clandestine

and without pouring
out the sloppy slump
predicted by beauties
of the moral novella

leave each undercut
to its lucky bleeding
and thrown measure
to its brightest place

*

Nb. a late fresh remark tumbling
flags stabbed in veneer taxing the list, the personal
overinflation from graphic ardour
and hardly persuasive so much as
grist to the classically worn tastes
Field Marshal Sir General Reader
upon the codex set bomb happy
integrity as only one who works
with words for a living who only
knows a trick of each thing then
drawn to attention on scaffolds
their high point and martial wit
scolds even soap upon dubbing
no buts but sights in sore morals
scampering back to an enclosure
           application pending
granted for spoke interpretation
but within age-old flattery sacks
ready for the latent norm in stills

onward trinitarian soldiers, mum's
the stumbling blue steel and cape
the night off from maps or sundry
but a sign of whose loss exactly

*

And in the consoling fabric
do *la fleuve*'s runny vowels
unbound to the dreams run
aground to darned abrasion
monstrous Roman progeny
of church and the latinate
long claws of what bookish
and reverent matrix in idols
the hints of doubling texture
one white space on another
as darkly bred punk gnosis
tittering in a plush back row
how gripe shouts delirium
and squeezes the syllabary
into the brood and comfort
ragdoll of its mislaid babies
one more linear B calculus
held up for the exemplary
how not to come on boyish
sundering bricolage raptors
with the FBI tyepwriter scan
churning over the merest em
and tithes of professionalism
as the rivers run fair to dry
parchment burning up isles
dropped to palling scripture
recycling its bloody run-on

*

So much for the plain sung champagne moment
            whose rebuked unicorn tendency
            shows up an uncanny free crony
            still laxer somehow in interview
                        the veil flaring trench
            spread among unbelieving scores
            turned to his beatific tooth crown
            and with so much fertile pasture
            positive sciences aching to seed
            why spoil the dividend with any
            but the general's special flavour
            with a crux set upon such cracks

                        *

    Seen from under a hooded ravage cape
    the maths given out formal tyrannies

    are smuggled praxis in figures no more
    attuned to submission than divine parts

    turn another striking full grown feature
    staggering to dandy up frozen blooms

    but oh how crude in the azure parting
    the pocket princess out for number one

    and subfusc myrmidons drilled to an inch
    of sweet wrangling cue spent biology

                        *

            Flap of images sworn
            browning another purr
            now warships slip sail

gone to trawl all grim
number and dead prices
poisoning the reserve

upon door long blame
and the old score cloak
flighty proof to dismal

then catastrophe loops
bending on the arabic
over crescents of zero

*

The minus carried on under your eyes
how the free scoring knows no fermata

but strips to a lightfast and rakish lap
before the men from influence studies

show how liberal they are with the dead
and the darkest circles turn back summers

then whack one off the list on an index
to share in bruising with what held it up

or so the poor soul drowns in catalogues
whatsoever trimmed from empty sets

*

No more to sing Achilles
not a wrath bowl in strife
and frost dogs on shame

for all that falling spoils
tablets to lime composed
war on word fur on worse

the names we cannot sing
but no the scroll lays the
fatal stretch in huffy lays

stiff in etched epaulettes
shaking in a bloody sash
that softly crows of pain

*

Not, then, to subsist upon possessions
        struck by the fixed run and crime
                in which aptness trembles
                as much as the purest cold
once quipped of as slight technicians
                turning character to exact
                the fray in bold, as when
                the burst into luminosity
                is no more a cheap rigour
it merely shows silhouettes of the unloved
                or as pulses set showering
                again finds curtains wanting
                where science is dead right
                and dead to the ensuing leak
it strikes a dying cloud found monstrous
                in a sort of fading caprice
                who smells sabotage in any
                question of reasoned traces
                there chilled in engineering
to testify how the structures can encroach
                and do the organism's will
                even spread to infections

because they become real
and become the particular
as if there the concepts are natural language
spread like a canopy over
an index of what gives out
a most culling fiery mantra

*

The call is dirty news
so feathered barking
to curve from shaggy
then savagery bland

again sweet stricture
bold as bright rains
done for bludgeoning
and all is quite through

the fang still showing
how sliver-tip proofs
take each gut or lyre
on quatsch or starch

for a speeding rubble
come formalist loves
then rip from a heart
a frond and its spleen

*

Knives rig up low-grade freight
to massage percentages, glory
shrunk from psycho modelling

that the prevailing gorse glows
in nature's bountiful brackets
        and animal symmetry

from out a sinister parenthesis
formula hundreds and thousands
dawn finds a puzzler fraternity
insulting vitalism's cartridge
then gone to tiny round robins
        in a losing regime

or whole crumbs gone to drips
shaving in a blazing dipthong
contra to some cubic songster
as painting to sparkling dogs
are a worrying kind of abstract
        in the pastoral wax

but the bloody park takes off
showing mathematical beauty
for a contradiction in terms
how willed to hustled brevity
runs up and really good to go
        springs into ruin

                *

Before numbered among weather reports
yet more footnotes to the arc plausible

be a good little soldier be some flaw
squalid state then ribbons spun to disarm

new ripped influence with gassy breaches
how long is the garden of double standards

when the atomic dog goes off on branches
that's the figurine cut to breathing in

and you must not think of live refulgence
or feathered detours through London leaves

*

Rough as innumerable wound
then wail and drip locution
off loving hides quite false
while new blood conceals

a lead thorn veiling tyranny
is number and legion in the
long grass with not a bean
burnt on thy furrowed brow

nothing but bubbling under
spoken of as light exercise
a streak of *argutezza* rising
to all the trawl and so forth

*

One more gantry which cannot be excluded
worrying the corpse formerly known as law

nor the shade seeking data without persons
the trace of the first harbour left to balloon

into the powerful part of the old argument
tripping off the flush box marked as *local*

while belting out concrete but empty sets
though of course all but for the purposes

of this million times fitter than some germ
shuffling one more zero through the needle

*

Prank shame rising
burns ice berg uplit
from flowing locks
turning loop scree

figure and end torn
the smile sun melts
who arrives for the
triple win bonus tip

upon dank defection
and so fills the arch
of the sent is a dune
brigade turning files

*

As on a night thrown upon glass houses
minimalist pah not minimal enough

and scarcely a dissonant squawking parp
but scenery chewed to dusty prancing

amid the half-baked smoke and monitor
to the counter-what is it caterwauling

blissed out in reverb to all lost vulgars
who shivers a square dance latin circled

to infinite dawns of the blandest regress
the kitsch done just so and not even kitsch

*

Stein   meets   the   Beach   Boys
        umm   perhaps   more   hash   browns
than   double   meaning   and   fast
        refried   bibles   of   camping   shine
whose   still   sedans   sedately   purr
        that's   pacing   streamed   to   files
the   démarche   trills   eyes   right
        and   smile   before   livers   singe
for   omens   in   noodling   spools
        36   minutes   and   you're   cool
and   relax   this   won't   take
        classics   sans   class   sans   high
modern   minus   tears   or   cyclorama
        where   springs   that   long   line
now   oh   caroline   no   now
        empty   is   the   suffering   gone
where   bled   the   youth   truce
        it   differs   the   pony   power
under   barrage   in   cowbell   heaven
        were   there   become   numbers   and
as   some   who   were   there
        but   not   with   it   there
were   left   smiling   but   cooler

*

But to return the stark strain
shields even loving strangers
who lie stretched over canvas
and remark how pure as pure

driving rain breaks the cover
out of fresh eye and best left
as in a certain sense the thing
is become quite another calm

not to be sewn up for brands
so says the aporia merchant
on a rare stroke crashing bore
that can ill afford its civilian

but cut throat by appointment
come the purpling exponents
and cultural studies crawling
over every little fruitful gross

*

How do the virgin nine
plot their blowsy rags
so said souls unfurled

marbling biscuit runes
gone stale then reveal
violls so softly plucked

as all quite arctic sent
come off it sow & muse
it's pile and sally tyre

burnt to thermal sponge
or dagger strewn awe
flourishing ruby altars

*

Scales have at first the figure
and extent of the cuticular
let them eat small pastries

pronounces its sugary balm
over encircling mediators
all made to break the wind

and lay on your gold leaf
ribbing the glass window
pebble breath done quarry

diagonal terracotta weaves
such calculated ornaments
and formalism out of sorts

*

Whose shards are but aftermaths spilt
and tendered beyond the limits
of so-called concrete univerals
where concrete matches the cut
beneath a heavy paddling foot
now sense done for in speculative congress
how a dice-throwing fraternity
holds soft to shoot the bruise
in cherished briefs or thongs
the hazard in its quality razor
just as precursors haunt the dying collection
with thumb prints, dimensions
etched into a scheming motto
how much, how long, how on
with the still cult and lineage
and this is indeed hardly the bacchanalian
spent inserting a geometry
come stations of the plaque

unspeakable then so restless
on a relic done to time lines
with all eyes on the sparkling bottom line
when Mammon met Kylie
or some other poetic shower
for belated sparks of their
language game that is none
and never a game doing its texture on you
but the birth of its discretion
that would be late or singular
and out beyond the numbers

*

Till right when you thought ah the nadir
inquisition difference turning no noes

yet cannot take to beatings darkly tamped
beyond even the nihilist's most refined

reluctance to goose said flaps of irony
was is so concrete as to form a place

and not the sheer jaw-dropping quadratics
that tat could so fester the belief squeeze

whose strange beauty is a dead cat bounce
now that the bar is lower than rarebit

*

Spent face and calamity
quite bit to sullen pence
ent price and vaunt dice

vowel to decree nought
what price obsolescence
who would but bone up

and deep soul soft soap
for concept provenance
were the *the* to actual

so sweeps the plastic
palm spar or rapt carpet
as a bark sped to bronze

*

Every best guess hedges the back and forth
on each person table and spindling pulsar

gliding on what misses from out spelt pads
on a full set of digits two up two down

bunks in its element and who'd be that pelt
with stifled babies living the floor boards

how many and asunder show up through-puts
driving each proper break down mighty

on spam satin arrays spooning spooning
and against touch tones doing their own thing

*

Pale   face   warrior   bled   wry
    how   much   the   hormone   balls
sweet   gripe   or   fasces   revolver
    barrelling   the   laugh   torn   wrist
then   fist   blank   and   subborned
    one   Sunday   wept   candy   star
who   takes   plays   dead   lion
    saddled   over   the   picket   medic
saner   come   bunker   of   choice
    how   grazing   gives   the   Nissen
that   shudders   for   bomb   gruel
    rubbed   in   sky   white   impasto
then   sulks   cold   dewy   sump
    buttered   not   bussed   or   yoked
before   the   lesson   seeps   through
    its   entropic   brush   down   strophe
looped   round   each   marbled   fear
    that's   gasp   how   low   dispirited
the   wretch   picked   on   punishing
    schemes   marked   out   for   scumble
after   the   fashion   and   sweatshop
    now   your   streak   born   arguing

*

Firmly among munchkin
shavers the little seconds
but not quite firing on all

the picturesque middens
for the broker shed gloss
one to one draw comfort

then the telegraphed pass
for some scandal armour
it is just chunky knitting

the crippling debt to sun
leaking phlegm and swan
weaving mulch in its nest

*

Another one Mr totality
gags fend off the image
of chlorofluorocarbons
done chip from blocked

links held above glassy
ceilings and simple blue
that nibbling at blinding
rope feed sans witness

who eats away the sky
from the definite article
under her grieving but
still swashbuckled halo

then chaps the backpack
one more heart warming
bolt on fractal odd bod
then blips for the spent

*

And flexed to dispell non-intuitive quanta
come graffito off snazzy bruises who yelps

for a man with a wand sleaving it sleaving
what margin then is this so purple edge

recalled to flee its fresh limit come zoom
in stretchers or bones up the crack canvas

so shiftily bowling the crush and scything
elbows and each train to commuting drift

into the repellents beyond cut borders
or humanly burnt into unravelled clothes

*

Disenchanted
at the getting
edge to smile
scarper dusts

shirk the gory
and das Volk
now showing
Euclid alone

gazing on her
bare beauties
when madame
simian twister

to lark or guts
then a wrench
do but lay off
ye silver dogs

*

The lozenge, the triangle, the egg:
        strung out finite to scorching c/o
        vulgar idealism in transfiguration
        dirty anastasis from quick impress
        in which slow brushes fall fallow
        to moss or licks of a daily plunge

placed at a door marked perpetual accumulation
clouds of words as slogans bursting into soul
     or some ogre flayed into vitality
     when slurry dries out its figurine
     impasto for the surgeon doing
     the sphere the cone the cylinder
     encircling mantlepiece decorum
     in plasters subsiding for gravity
     or prisons of hot point literalism
     in fresh talk of sexing the trinity
pneuma on heat so naked in a modalist dawn
that rust drips wishes for nomina as numina
     numbered stars drizzled in oils
     painted over an inisidous gloss
     with parent child and paraclete
     striking Arian flavours in a mix
     glued to yours truly the parsing
     rapiers among the substantives
     air-brushed to mockney monsters
     of a synoptic gospel whose merest
     mention sends up budding artistes
     how the whirlpool exaggerates
          with the spirit as a bird
          mired in the accostings
          on pain of triangulation
          and dissolving plumage

*

     Turbulent to pitched gloat
     or half way to accounting
     where rugs like diagrams
     double in evening charms

the repeat take arabesque
at face value and argues
for the two state solution
each strip of taken earth

spelt out along trig points
while *sorry* opens more
square brackets than death
as though the sheer weight

makes a critique of resolve
and the state shadowed by
lost amends in the blaming
as though origins mattered

*

The books withdrawn for spat marginalia
down hollows of laddered falling falling

encore for the budgetary rabbit paddle
one more nebula rising another star utensil

curling to autumn compost and so composed
before more congestion for tiring tiring

cut a divider into sleep now stretched
on the canvas whose will to skeleton

would shed the bed sores of the horizon
and leave only dawn to its ashen grips

*

Abstractly conceived
        as slave ships swoon
in the baptismal broth
        idem to indifference
ground out in axioms
        principled to a gunner

thus one more tapering apex
        signor pyramid smiling
at his heroic divertissement
        that and concepts of being
snug in the good dip stupor
        before knifed by theories

or for the ripped under belly
        shoulder ham trembling
calling occidental deference
        or who dares doffs
to the massing missiles
        and by nature porous

till flipsides show raw blood
        thrown the lights of oil
and a queue of martyrs
        set for stoning or bored
with mooning scripture
        set to bronze in exile

*

Low screen numbers lift up in vortices
as the orange hums that liquid resolves

or sing the cut edges of wash and slip
in strangling turns the wreck of the duvet

polished and ironed by the architecture
where sinks in marshy woollens how order

couples with property rights and sleepers
rumbling over rails do steady whispers

all prepped and primed above slated echoes
and the mother of all crackling plasters

*

Sweeter as rivetting iron
one heroic damp patch
lifts the whole ensemble

and threshes on in steam
so allow me quoth Sancho
you are chained to a wall

the rest is sleep and then
pebbles amid the tyrant's
calculus who would shrug

off bonds until well clear
of fact's autumn flowering
where daggers breed limbs

*

White walls bleeding, inked for bitter tort
            ripping doves to lime, the more
            the struggle, the more belimed
            till set once more to fluttering
    gridlock and false dawn in-powred
    or in-blown keying in the net gross
    whole volumes of rude stuff taking

to commodities like a triune abacus
       the lost aches of avian cinema
       and its younger technologies
       going pale well before its time
leaving well what else but leaving
the body politic stripped to biscuits
singing cakes suicided to humanism
       a merest well-tempered squeak
       sounding civics or skulduggery
       cue the priests trading in death
even to bonded stars in arks rampant
breeding -nesses, -tudes, and –ties
plurals out of lucid intervals yawning
between initial stock and future crop
how worth is if in motion and only if
       then in price wars the dusters
       in a cleaning regime of grief
       with food for the passing rats
       or poisons breeding antidotes
       to box office and pension but
        all calculations are off

       *

White then as peace
can be in the account
of stank equilibrium

and soft as the birds
nor rightly summons
but as near to piercing

the pain shield checks
and profession in pink
till the fibres compose

and fat busting chances
take on its oxymoron
over the consoling stats

*

How crawling glazes blister into night
then one day or another it will break

from days docked into a passion of clocks
and even out the bonding counterfeit

where more to its curvy than opts to turn
out winded nimbly under evening's cowl

then gone on end on to dancing quadrants
one even and then pretty much another

though never oddly the quirk left ironing
its stock of lean years drawn to infinites

*

Stringer curbs
bloom & flake
and you plump
for guess turf

to blow in face
a non-intuitive
piggy sort code
trickling blouse

damp sparklers
and wind gown
shivering goose
slip and bumper

*

Squaring up over from left-handedness
measured out in traces floored by stupor

who can but spell out cod labour and scores
upon scores to the paper's scarred profit

how even's not the barrier it once seemed
once broken into marching mezzanines

come threads and tanks set upon embracing
conceptual veneers with precision skies

there regulars set to bridge the triumph
and spring lists of things not done by morning

*

How old rain gives a chill around the socks
but so soon trembled by cooking and ashes

or just killing its brief arch till evening
where supple tankers do modern muses

stewing for treasure the opening soils
their matinée and pale models passing

how its gag of love rips your very ear
to tides and murders shuffled and banking

so the power blows then evens up logs
over a smokeless dune that skin turns dry

*

Gone cold upon the incoming swarm
    or flung back to prime flux
    how swaggering multitudes
    will freshen up absolution
but come out to show out whom pacify
    their flags of convenience
    the good ship counterfeit
    tuned contra sung dances
now grids encircled till breaking diction
    how public rebel yell boy
    in would-be slime mould
    turns against pall bearing
each to their own private money lung
    or yet bled to rehearsals
    where the finite armies
    harden to callous scores
it is a bad infinity for finite friends
    when nature calls or off
    bred to within an ounce
    of this life, this massing
down corridors in which idealism stalks
    and you are bound upon
    such laughing matters as
    one such among so many

*

So brush up in sweeping
statements re the degree
in the sacrosant dailies
with blurbs turning dust

such coverage sans phrase
scrambling in the labours
just leaping little dangers
of which to least can need

done oh bread run blusher
on waves held to bosom
the fighting talk and cuff
in a prelude to brochures

first exhibit turning brisk
inert manger in one eye
on both ends in creases
said vested and such like

*

Another speculative good Friday
now starring improved tyranny
set to get one over on the money
somewhere between the sensible
and the curse of a curdling shade

or beached upon summer graphs
free to reckon with no family tree
viz. a mathematician hell bent on
disproving the trinity against the
god-botherer versed in fuzzy logic

till a triumphant queuing system
turns the probable into trolley rage
as when the number crunching set
truly decline their pre-paid tickets
for the massacre of the innocents

*

Another socking half hour until toughs
fall into rough details still forthcoming

with no can do put beyond open fruits
that livid night preens the angled pillow

what with cruel mercies set upon the shelf
and more aid shrubbery in star chambers

than how the savour calculus turns pale
or what in semi-detached folkish stains

can ground out or beckon in the cameras
and catch bleeding dust after the thunder

*

As a book bleeds out of its broken spine
a cool look rubbed into a cross hatching

the rayons leaping out of one language
and the miserable fruits in sterile grafts

or the small of the back turned to cupping
slop and pall under cover of oceans

before breaking into spilling pallettes
that deck its unprimed bed of wilted flax

to the cut of the blundering currents
spelt out so each one speaks out of the wrong

*

So much of duration
to laugh answering
revolutions of spur
flame thrown once

on its tire the usual
periods thing or big
fruit so likewise by
single or slow tread

poring into the *field*
hardly lush to endure
but neat braced skein
for burning diagrams

elbow to finger grime
uh-huh my crunchers
wrinkling leather dash
under the masked raw

*

As another wave brushes each fibre
the wash tumbles and set upon bruises

it barely merits the nubile counters
as glasses cloud that once were in faces

etched then in the fallen reef and our years
its tender marbling struck to rosy spools

the brush of stacks practised in a contempt
that partly for that reason stands up loose

change and foul biting roughed up for stroking
but made clear once again a loathing puce

*

Quite literally little by little
       amid late digits whom glossy
that and DNA skirting blouses
       finds fine siblings triple fold
high above the lung cancel
       and the hard saying bastard

that being and nothing rhyme
       pooled once fur and leaky
till gripped in terror morsels
       a novella moon slow pasted
to bloom repeater point 99
       who would not sack cloth

the scam comfy or clutchy
       wrangled into cork nude folds
shone to scratch burnt moles
       where from boules weep nails
finger dipped in ocean salsa
       till later came stilling salt

*

But who would not hover in the grace
       between matters in the difference
       and the weakness of all argument
       that comes between the equation
       and the data held so circumspect
among the solutions that cannot be endured
       as the mangle resembles family
       turning in on summer snapshots
       cut into some stupid application
       as what matters starts to flare up

then as now shifting in food over the animus
             it can hardly tame the grammar
             built into our illusion of justice
             then strapped to the picnic sack
             that came and went in the night
but linger until the tidy balance is renounced
             where love would corrupt each
             file transferred to the private sect
             where genomes are but the maps
             and the holidays we never shared

                         *

             But the direct address to the serial
             name, rank and number remaining
             strangely silenced or in this respect
             the behaviour true to form and few

             it is indeed remarkable how daily
             and constant encounter bears upon
             moist reliance in concepts of whose
             possession yet content with its uses

             only passing acquaintance by name
             the alien slave valued at mute face
             can pass over on the homeland bus
             nor sprung from the rattle & shake

             but none will admit their belongings
             out by the hundreds in hypothetical
             and graphic lounge or figurative wig
             showering duty on tons of split land

                         *

How   come   the   no-no   metronome
     fallen   catchy   over   rugged   jugs
going   shunt   dumb   and   tetchy
     the   cow   poke   mini   cape
fiddling   stoles   strung   over   brows
     there's   nothing   will   fright   it
stone   scum   fangling   so   naked
     takes   the   wound   up   plaster
or   gulled   mode   stroke   mood
     all   gaudy   for   stocking   idols
the   toys   sweating   rank   vetch
     plimsoll   to   trainers   then   plasma
howling   a   hollow   pat   algebra
     re   daily   buffing   and   heaving
skips   silken   with   pitted   writs
     for   escarpment   of   the   brass
done   whiter   and   light   gawps
     a   very   cordial   bid   splendour
the   screeds   and   triune   render
     as   fondest   in   iron   diaphragm
sheds   yours   ever   square   wisp

*

A supreme note shines forth a uniform
suburb of how many glances gone south

the special touch of the habit and scarf
now the fourth wall inches a damp ruin

pouring forth stricken fields into carpets
and shower crops into a portrait frame

holding the peaceable upon the spent
tracers with autographed plungers of light

and a sense of proportion thrown up through
a streamed horizon in which love plunged

*

Hey fiddle the count
or the burnt creative
all the way to a rose
or budding metaphor

stripped of hedging
till the raw calculus
says hand over fist
in brief nasty brutish

and short arrays sing
dog the curt entrepôt
stay with me, stay the
buttoned toothy bulk

*

There is that finite lie so sandwiched
even built into the word creation
like the most benign young chef
fiddling while what was prepared
is what is now said to be sourced
between turning in on a bonfire of origins
but so prone to lavish its metrics
upon a profit calculus with such
dull soufflé in the coming proofs
and no fuel quite like sour charm

then hardly a day waltzes by in anything
        but the history of its accumulation
        fever to touch what smoking flesh
        that would eat itself rather than rest
        triumphant in a cosmopolitan dish
it is what makes it stick or wounded soul
        left for the dark birds to feed upon
        when graves call for dancing zip
        and whatever left in us owes zilch
        but force fed flirtations with work
as if bowing to abstraction could keep up
                off ancient spurs and spoils

                        *

When you fold in domestic burial
any detail of disturbance stares back

a puncture tailing out beyond the frame
on crowded grounds bled back in the dark

so that even an odd smiling kills light
and lolls forward upon a merging case

shut to seem tenuous with best practice
that turns into doors bearing up branches

who would plane down even all so fussy
out of solidarity with scare quotes

                        *

                Shine stark rotund
                does temper lunge
                viz. quantity throne
                has that form only

and merely a three
in one spatial tatty
yes that scar each
is limited to zoom

like it the quantum
yawn broke tender
an alp for a sphere
these pieces frank

opular column lists
the simply drying
and brazen coming
strips the pure idea

*

And there is no more speculative proposition
than the balletic claim that anything equals

anything else: viz. maths unequal to its own
claims as the very glitch previously gleaned

showers down honeyed fronds and cue dance:
splint hoop then rolling which withers doesn't

not counting the room now running on empty
verging on into purest essentials, the very cog

swung aloft in distant insight, blue to external
to the thing or things thus altered as its means

are shades constructed and in proof, in sum:
sublations so far inward in slum totals, how

neither concrete sense crowds nor even love
creams the least stretching lines of equality

till setting jessant falls short of its jeté mumble
and all in turns cloudy, crisp, yes scar rampant

*

Tis neon now fiery crush
on starkest smithereens
squealing come rest track
as beaming traces show

lost pay to moth masque
and smugger captions
beguile each shut lively
now sent beyond in furs

or go garland the wrath
dice in hot dashing rivet
with hammy drills racing
on old warp factor blush

hand to geld wax mouth
spangled to windscreen
diamonds gone to crown
its veil in mergent blue

*

The specs go finger tapping, heaps of fees
the peas in a row, singing
undo the fast and hand-packed slop of aid
all together now, blithe box
spread roughly over ladders, blue on blue
the thing heart cooling off

and wedded to spine-killing in wry slacks
       who even cares about no. 7
now give and gray showering in the dark
       to note a single absent dog
you, me and the clasp of far satellites
       tuned to gloating precedence
the feathery hatch with renewed gusto
       and so much for dualism

                    *

As the double sack fits the mendicant
       done to a yielding purée
in thousands so offered up for burning
       so stripped of muscle tone
the world of the *firstest* bursting its gut
       come slurry and ordinance
as number locks onto incoming souls
       the prosaic but bright light
spread to how floral leaflets of practice
       flow weary ways or waters
and how the mass destruction eagerly
       spreads its cynical umbrella
awaited with everything up in smoke
       and conventional weapons
in the latest mockery and cakewalk
       for an audience of one

                    *

Both burnt and dilating in the usual
and that in general the bottom edges

become divested from the ordinary
that things can nip in colouring malice

as would plainly meet as much in return
some dazzled cuff or a quick of trouser

but dragging nothing into view save sleep
while physical bulk weathers out the loss

as depicts your unseen profile or scream
begging for crosses to amount to less

*

How distant tribes became too rare
became a visitor's dark living room
or a mathematical sublime ambling
along some dull axiom of grievance
    shed to rifts
  upon the age of lost cities
  as an inventory held light
  took seals from flaking sky
  scribed by a second hand
  then axed bulk iron quality
  and set to brazen scalding
  arabesques and character
  arched over baptismal fire
    and so cutting
the glance seemingly overwhelmed
what with Pauline conversion going
head over heels for the hate speech
and bleeding knuckles without need
  of blunt circumcision
  but built like a citadel
  where the inward song
  goes beyond measure
  and becomes a subject
  bound to the marching
  turns of the letters sent

But no, that pathos has finally burst
and to speak of unsettling reassures

only a parched shower often counted on
as if blooming stains can be repainted

or overscore what will pass for coping
though nothing can ever settle again

whenever their crash breaks in a new sense
of what milder day or moulded harness

once mounted on rusting tracks of global
proportion and coats trailing capitals

*

Raw   spurious   then   scenery   floored
     creams   veiled   scrim   and   horns
cue   needy   frazzling   in   flights
     moments   how   naif   left   wagering
long   bows   and   longer   draining
     its   claw   dimming   to   pulses
skipped   down   to   tripped   blocks
     each   lost   measure   done   fêted
but   driven   the   swampy   stews
     past   flaying   or   flown   missiles
pearly   clams   and   straw   farce
     the   plafond   dyed   and   bleeding
once   fast   colours   found   wanting
     but   beached   where   stories   dissolve
toxins   in   each   anecdote   born
     as   landing   lights   spill   ruptures
across   unknown   but   echoed   folds

smothered   in   ghost   slash   copy
the   shout   punch   who's   counting
come   cropping   the   peeling   dune
then   spoilers   shorn   to   feints
parched   and   verging   on   barks
that   lapse   some   way   lapsing

*

Lozenges out of lousy slab tombstone
showing rectilineal planes, two acute

and two obtuse with a diamond rhomb
common to brilliants and roses why then

the theodicy of the self-styled *pure*
sticking with parties and faith in numbers

even irrational ones grown so absurd
their speculative wings melted to clippers

but strictly tuned to heraldic draughstmen
as gardens of virus make out each cell

*

And only the semantic
tongue fire persiflage
tucks a green goddess

into a bluff percentile
would the two stagers
take to strimmer dupe

crumbs upon crumble
from the top table and
as sticklers fall to beg

the shades shot from
a drop dead beret and
the glass is half empty

*

Thrown to rise upon yellowing paper
ups the massaging to graphic fibres

each sawn diskette chiselling fiery dust
in forgotten formats calling dead labour

furred up and quite broken to duration
but just as the bottom falls out of life

there but for the grace finds its pentagon
bonds as blank splits in the chilliest sky

and fallen as intimate scars of blue
so easily blown and yet to no floor

*

The trough implies some
        dimmer viz. the cool
latter retiring jinxed but
        who's to know spruce

so razor pink shirty
        when the image rind
dribbles curtains of ferocity
        all preened and verified

the true kiddy well
        spark that craving scheme
sunk flatly and bitter
        shines in gross cruise

over crowded jitters stooping
        where orange clearly huffs
who's the envy now
        spent brand spanking new

flutters to confetti caprice
        religion pants right enough
where great laxity speaks
        kinder there's much hostage

and group scruples huddling
        in said analyzer braid
branches shouting qui vive
        never mind which pique

*

Territory fired
out of the hides
and parchment
still to scrolling

but even alight
is no single file
nor even temper
but a spending

and then a face
scarred in lines
saying nothing
nor even entreats

only a quick fix
the still in view
varnished and lit
by satellite states

*

Past   caring   downs   in   coughs
   phillipic   spelt   rough   to   despond
chewed   then   rude   spools   rhubarb
   well   more   schizo   gone   thermidor
before   the   growth   catches   craven
   high   cult   flummery   and   downs
then   drawn   fluid   seeding   flighty
   and   among   them   shout   cheese
the   crock   stubble   soup   undone
   gives   out   thumb   cuffed   notes
rippling   a   worth   frazzling   purse
   in   fennel   saying   charred   beam
flip   top   hedges   and   landing
   ladies   mistaking   yet   another   dead
snatching   at   how   what   went
   pubface   just   shat   on   goods
with   the   noble   loss   cymbal
   getting   off   on   infinite   syntax

*

Figure one quoth bastard
with sharp pointy stick
as all the yards run quick

and cup screaming leave
it is heavier to meet the
dribbling sideburns and

pooling draff to swarm
the ledgers taking count
and lighter to shuddering

its spent tremble in beads
which shun the dragon boy
in his song of dungeons

                    *

And abandons fruity coughs
            beneath the phrase lime
how glass eyes make over
            each spare tucked atom
from whose spilling orchestra
            shoots triple headed rules

come fine jewel shorting
            daft for machine sticks
or swords of modest petal
            ravished puts things proud
with euphonic porn parades
            the lofty key grazing

back come mirrored stocks
            each from lightened loads
the ancient lyric shuffle
            sprained by cold quoting
that stroke steer derided
            her ethos stirring liquids

                    *

Still comes quick billing
down grafts fairly sterile
the prodigal sung surplus
strikes awe then resumes

its lessening stale ellipsis
fortressed for the duration
like strangers and alloyed
antiques of civilian ardour

the dimming left uneven
boned and plucked scraping
now blanker shone grounds
showing feather to sunny

least middles in disputes
called stupid and singled
out from franker foliage
that dance for oblivions

obliging a fried snapshot
and most finite protocols
so jubilant for slipstreams
among the receding lines

AFTERMATHS

'Your last proportion is that of figure, so called for that it yields an ocular representation, your meeters being by good symmetrie reduced into certaine Geometricall figures, whereby the maker is restrained to keepe him within his bounds, and sheweth not only more art, but serveth also much better for briefenesse and subtiltie of device.'

Puttenham, *The Arte of English Poesie*

'This conflict between the general form of the proposition and the unity of the Notion which destroys it is similar to the conflict that occurs in rhythm between metre and accent. Rhythm results from the floating centre and the unification of the two. So, too, in the philosophical proposition the identification of Subject and Predicate is not meant to destroy the difference between them, which the form of the proposition expresses; their unity, rather, is meant to emerge as a harmony.'

Hegel, *The Phenomenology of Spirit*

'The effort that is required to grasp new music is not one of abstract knowledge, nor is it one of acquaintance with some systems or other, with theorems, much less with mathematical procedures. It is essentially imagination, what Kierkegaard called the speculative ear...'

Adorno, *Essays on Music*

Few things are more disappointing than apologies disguised as theoretical confessions. Apologies nevertheless seem called for, even at the risk of lessening otherwise necessary resistances to public taste. But let slip the dogs of articulation and there are costly tithes to be paid to the gods of utilitarianism heralded by the armies of capital. Who would not true infotainment see, come hype or academic audit. Demands for promotional paraphernalia can then be acknowledged as interrogative tortures set on consigning what would be public to the long arms of private property relations. One response to the invasive protocols of publicity and identification is that recommended to prisoners of war: acknowledge only name, rank and serial number. No blurbs, no pack-drill: and no pretence at fireside chats with the armchair generals.

Resistances weaken in the face of sustained interrogation, but the anxiety of the merest title, pseudonym or mnemonic is reflected in the honour accorded to the anonymity of the unknown soldier and the unsung legends of dead labour. Even if titles seem like a sorry vestige of privilege or, better still, Adamic hubris, there is more than a tincture of puritan self-congratulation evidenced by works announcing themselves as beings without allegiance, kin or title – untitled, *sans titre, ohne Titel* – or as beings of merely numerical classifications such as opus numbers and their attendant chapters, pages, opuscules, sub-sections, enjambments, ceasuras and so on to the dawn of infinite shade. They flee from me that sometime heard each call to frozen postures amid the sordid machinations of interior decor.

Between the demands of vocation, conscription and commodification, the limits of what can be professed by way of oeuvre offer as much room for generous reconstruction as the humane interrogator affords victims. Once executed, the corpse can look forward to virtual graveyards scattered among the fields of socially divided labours. Without some indication of willed or intuitive prejudices, it is perhaps too much to expect anyone to understand, beyond dutiful recognition, what might have been implied but is constrained to remain *sub judice*. Against seals of arithmetical identification, however, there is something to be said for the unlikely possibility that prisoners reveal more than they intend or can sum up. Not so much, then, between the lines, blanks in the breach or *sous rature*, but in the flight from the law of unwitting oversights where vision loses the privilege of hieratic divination and all the theological regimes of reading eager to supply the relevant ordinance, but would rather no more than as set down to the immanent torque, the productive bents so framed by restricting confession to acknowledgments of due process.

Beyond inevitable testimonies to the historical conditions of contemporary production, not least defeats of reason in the face of the new global imperium, the above writings thus owe some of their genesis to a reflexive restlessness with the tyranny of number and of psuedo-mathe-matical procedures in the making of art. Whereas the modern world of prose revels in its supposed freedom from formality, tradition suggests that mathematical patterns of various kinds are conditions of the pos-sibility of art, perhaps most explicitly in Pythagorean conceptions of music and the physics of sound. As Adorno once suggested, every triad that a composer still uses today already sounds like a negation of the dissonances that have meanwhile been set free. But soft, hear the songs of mass destruction come marching in who speak of quantum mechan-ics and unfurling radiation over the desert sky.

Between the extremes of avowedly intuitive and non-intuitive approaches to musical form, recent works developed out of the shadow of totalised compositional technique and post-minimalist whimsy indi-cate an impasse analogous to difficulties in other arts. It is not unmedi-ated accession to the qualities and angles of the sphere, thing or object-ball that animates the recurrence of diverse, largely automatic acts of *wannabe* recognition. Much of what passes for minimalism might more accurately be understood as ironic literalism, the knowingly monoto-nous formalism in which all cows are indeed cows, but if and only if seen as such. Conceptualism is no less literal-minded, recycling received ideas rather than engaging with anything quite so conceptual as the con-cept itself. There is nevertheless a necessary negativity at work in such isms, even if not with the epochal largesse beloved of paradigm-shifters. As a negative principle, the spirit of the letter abjures the autonomy of positivistically misconceived hermeneutics or philology, and when the letter exceeds even the claims of aesthetic spirit, this is not positive transcendence but wrung violation.

The heroic avant-garde succeeded in hollowing out the dignity of spec-ulative identification. Affirmative synchronicities – such as myth and modernity, freedom and harmony, love and prosody – are revealed as category mistakes rather than engaging ruins of spirit. See history to mathematics fly, now vainly gaze, turn giddy, rave and die. One of the unintended consequences of avant-garde ambition is the pervasive pleas-ure taken in reductive but avowedly radical forms of contextualisation, from situationism to cultural studies. Oscillations between purification and transgressive collation fall victim to the abstract identity of purity and impurity. Pure maths is no less impure, uncertain, or plain useless than the most pure compositional formulae. Calls for aesthetic autonomy and for the radicalism of tradition are sung from the same messy hymn sheet, as if the costume of the globe were Galileo's *Great Book of the World*, with its silent discourse charactered by triangles, circles and other geometrical figures, and as if writing were scripture or the handwriting of some god.

Much rests on the viability of projective appropriation through strategies of phenomeno-logical reduction, from the supposed politics of formal innovation to the wounded allegories of sensuous damage, or from witty but sceptical dramatisations of parallel universes to ironic disavowals of recognised necessity. Einstein could not believe that God played dice, and yet it is more suprising still to find so many residues of secular superstition at the end of the line. What seems hard to acknowledge amid the reduction of aesthetic intentionality to strategies of restless differentiation, micro-differentiation and nihilistic irony – all the various hymns to difference, to the Other and to the quasi-transcendental impossibility of reconciliation – are the underlying affirmations accruing as the determinate consequences of so much scepticism and negativity. Herein lie the traceries strung out by the phenomenology of *anti-geist* or anti-spirit.

Art carries on like some beautiful soul that neither affirms nor denies its complicity with the engagements it lovingly prolongs. One of the many ruses by which the spirit of speculation is bracketed or continued by other means is the embrace of mathematical reason – arm in arm and row on row, till legs are cut to logs and ribbons – but recognising this hardly frees speculation from the gambles invested in it. Terrible things have been done in the name of breaking with the tyranny of compositional hierarchies and so much painting by numbers. Blanched formalisms have proclaimed the triumph of chance procedures, as if improvisation could be more than a merely negative freedom to tinker with standards thereby reinscribed. Constitutive binaries – according to which synthetic compositions with hubristic ambitions oppose the differentials of free play – leave a broken middle where once dwelt content.

As if to confirm the resulting conformities, it is often hard to tell whether strained disjunctions are produced according to an underlying scheme or according to a logic of what might again be called accidents. The most classically schematic forms were animated by a forrest of accidentals just as the most romantically fluid organisms were often blind to the enclosure movements and agricultural mechanics enabling their pastoral fancies. If polemics more often become tedious bookends – prologues and epilogues to be ignored by all but the accountants of the imagination – then recent developments suggest the triumph of accountancy at the heart of the social text.

Put differently, there is no more speculative proposition than the claim that anything equals anything else. Even this statement errs towards the romance of tautological evasion, a chiasmus too far. Metaphor toys with the speculative rewards of identification, but lacks the legislative grammar demanded of rationality. Mathematics, for example, is not equal to its own claims. The rebuke is not new. Plato put into Socrates' mouth the observation that even those who are only slightly conversant with geometry will not dispute us in saying that this science holds a position the very opposite from that implied in the language of those who practise it. More recently, Daniel E. Styer notes that physicists are often clumsy in their use and understanding of quantum mechanics's central concepts, indeed they are protected from them by a screen of mathematics. What once ventured forth as processual *mathesis* becomes the reified calculus of administration, a logic of numerical sameness screened from nihilistic relativity. Negation is no less unequal to the task of speculative scepticism, especially in any inquiry into the poetics of experience seeking to delimit the phenomenological illusions involved in recourse to number as the mood, or will to power, of aesthetic reason.

Hegel is perhaps the harshest critic of the defective cognition of which mathematics is so proud. He declares that in mathematical cognition insight is an activity external to the thing it thus alters. The means employed, construction and proof, no doubt contain true propositions, but the content is false. With non-actual things like the objects of mathematics neither concrete sense-intuition nor philosophy has the least concern. This least cries out for attention, but why the righteousness of pure maths among its adherents? From the perspective of the damage done, mathematics is a form of biological tyranny, an anthropomorphic fiction no more divine or deserving of submission than any other biological form. Insofar as such tyrannies take hold of social action, the logic of capital and its military shield represent the priority of numeracy over literacy, of counting over the Heraclitean river. Even this metaphorical displacement calls on a frame in which the apex drawn into the middle distance claims its own theatrical geometry, as if the landscape could be so singled out and captured for intuition. As Barthes puts it, the stage is the line which stands across the path of the optic pencil, tracing at once the point at which it is brought to a stop and, as it were, the threshold of its ramification. Thus is founded – against music (against the text) – *representation*.

Writ large, there is a struggle between *logoi* and *mathemata* which maps graphs over the living expression of being and its speculative life in language. When has maths not been an adjutant in the massacre of the innocents? Contrary to the hopes of cubism, such as those intimated by Apollinaire, geometry is to painting as dogs are to sheep. The staging of geometry so as to encircle the nude model staring back is more candidly betrayed by Manet's *Le Déjeuner sur l'herbe*. Lest this be taken awry, the pastoral fantasies of abstract expressionism suggest that it is not really shepherds or sheep that pull the strings. Berating the stretched canvas for its supporting role is only a way of worrying sheepish illusions with intimations of materialism. The axis of the fourth wall assumes the domestication of what would be more open air passages through political music, a problem for which the conditions of representation cannot be ruled architectonically. Mathematical beauty is a contradiction in terms. The beauty of contradiction, moreover, rests in the ruin of form's will to power. The succinct quality of great equations does not justify hymns to formalism.

As Husserl once quipped, the mathematician is not really the pure theoretician, but only the ingenious technician. Heidegger boldly pointed out that mathematical knowledge is no more rigorous than philological-historical knowledge. It merely has the character of exactness. In its radical unity, the trinitarianism of science's world-projection brings a luminous simplicity and aptness, and beyond that – nothing. The nothing – what else can it be for science but an outrage and a phantasm? One thing is sure, science wishes to know nothing of the nothing. Nihilation will not submit to calculation in terms of annihilation and negation. Unspeakable experiments have been conducted along such lines. Adorno also highlights the way the primacy of mathematics reduces the question of meaning to a sort of faded, technical thought activity. As he puts it, the mathematician smells sabotage to the machinery in any question of meaning. The mathematician is concerned with ideal objects like the paleontologist is concerned with fossils.

Heisenberg provides chilling evidence that the *concern* of the scientist's objectivity confuses objective truth with social engineering. He admits, for example, that the power of natural and technical sciences has fundamentally changed the conditions of life on earth, but suggests that whether one calls it progress or danger, one must realize that it has gone far beyond any control through human forces. According to him, one may rather consider it as a biological process on the largest scale whereby structures active in the human organism encroach on larger parts of matter and transform it into states suited for the increasing human population. Substitute *one* with a vain particular disguising its will to power as a universal recognition and you have a pocket calculator with which to perform ideology critique. What one *is* becomes the integral calculus of social being, an entry in the index of worldly prose whose appendices are taking over the asylum. Where on Olympus is there a telescope capable of magnifying oversights into overviews? Who will educate such educators if the species is so conceived as if the organism were passively suited to statistical lies?

Heisenberg even suggests that it may take many years to distinguish truth and error, but finally the questions will be decided, and not by scientists but by nature itself, as if scientific ideas only spread like a true fungus. It is strange how the theory of relativity and its perspectival aporia lend themselves to the dogma that science still knows best. Heisenberg concedes that an important feature of the development of modern physics is the experience that concepts of natural language, vaguely defined as they are, seem to be more stable in the expansion of knowledge than scientific language. Apparently, for him, the concepts of natural language are formed by more immediate connections with reality, as if language could be natural, and as if the attempt to idealize science in and through language were not the expression of forces doing violence to their own otherwise unacknowledged temporizing and unnatural history.

Seen more generously, the objects of mathematics are merely ideal objects on which to waste free moments. What matters is the difference between an equation and the data it would circumscribe. Transfer to the *private* sector of the mathematical mapping of the human genome corrupts the meaning of *data* and threatens humanity with yet more creative accounting. The way creativity is over-rated reflects the alienation of finite spirit, the natural history built into the word *creation*. Where humans are concerned, the straightest line between two points requires dialectical thought. Families, friends and lovers continually demonstrate the stupidity of applying arithmetic to situations that matter: mathematical solutions cannot be endured. The theorem that the sum of the angles of a triangle is equal to two right angles takes no account of love triangles or the triune shape of spirit. And what can the spirit of geometry offer an inquiry into Proclus, for whom the truly existent has the trinity of beauty, truth and symmetry. Despite protestations of innocence among recent exponents of trinitarianism, Hegel remains the unthought condition for understanding how the Christian mysteries were rendered incomprehensible to understanding and how reason now comprehends their speculative and historical revelation.

Meanwhile, Kepler's ambition to show that the heavens are a kind of clockwork has its own half-life in the continuing way in which the humanism of the analogue clock is underestimated. The claim that

Dirac's equation predicted how almost half of all material existence at the time of the so-called *big bang* was made up of antimatter suggests that purveyors of popular science should read more Zeno. God may have been a remarkable mathematician, but whether the theology is Platonic or astrophysical, the ideas of before and after built into creationism are mathematical illusions better understood as grammatical fancies. Mindful, perhaps, of the violence of geometrical method in thinkers such as Descartes and Leibniz, Hobbes and Spinoza, Kant observed that nothing has been more harmful to philosophy than the imitation of mathematics, but forgot to mention the harm done mathematics by imitating itself. Just as Schlegel declared that a good preface is at once the square root and the square of its book, so a good aphorism shrugs off the desire for symmetry and merely mathematical balance. Afterwords become the bad infinities of hindsight. Schlegel also declared that publishing is to thinking as the maternity ward is to the first kiss: so the poem is to its aftermaths. While bullets fly and caterpillar tracks hum to the rhythms of blue grass, poems dream of more edifying occasions, more edifying even than the workshops and dissection laboratories of sundry literary geneticists.

There is no account adequate to describe the reification of everyday life according to accountancy: the calculus of profit makes for dull reading. As David Harvey has suggested, space and time have to be understood as social metrics produced through capital accumulation. Enthusiasts of telecommunication have even claimed that geography is history. But the symptoms of convergence within capitalist idealism are fuelled by a totality of antagonistic differentiation that would eat itself rather than rest triumphant in a cosmopolitan empire. The other projected into its final frontier is also its self-inflicted wound, the essence of what makes it tick. The attempt to reduce music to maths nevertheless shows the wisdom of birds who sing on without deference to human perception or to the paralyzed abstractions of numerical negativity. Similarly, in the era of its global diffusion, lyric's social metrics pretend to fall in love with numerical quantities so as to disguise fragile flirtations with the latest catastrophe.

In his meditations on metaphysics after Auschwitz, Adorno gives restless testimony to the historically conditioned enormity of the situation. Our metaphysical faculty is paralyzed because events have shattered the basis on which speculative metaphysical thought could be reconciled with experience. Quantity recoiling into quality scores unspeakable triumphs. But such provocations are themselves wagers mortgaged upon speculative delimitations of experience. Beckett went for broke: ... *nothing more restful than arithmetic, in a hundred thousand, in a million, it's too much, too little, we've gone wrong somewhere, no matter, there is no great difference here between one expression and the next, when you've grasped one you've grasped them all, I am not in that fortunate position, all, how you exaggerate, always out for the whole hog, the all of all and the all of nothing, never in the happy golden....* But satire is wasted on mathematical process because the codes involved lack the moral fibre for humour or reform. There is more to language, however, than the witty metamorphoses of binary codes. What *is* is more than grammar makes it seem. Even this *more* is more or less a logical shape or tendency, rather than an abstract quantity. It might be described as an inclination towards the parallel identity of finite and infinite being.

One of the ancient spurs to mathematical ingenuity was the desire to divide loaves of bread fairly, but it is a mistake to confuse justice with equal shares. Great political slogans, such as *From each according to their abilities, to each according to their needs*, point beyond mathematics to the spirit of recognition. Wisdom sees that justice is more than the sum of sentences and compensation packages: judgment is an art, not mathematical juggling. Speculative poetics transgress the limits of concrete sense-intuition without succumbing to fantasies of mathematical infallibility, exactitude or universality, but critics all too often behave like estate agents who do. As Beckett noted, literary criticism is not book-keeping. Proponents of non-intuitive poetics might try to claim Mallarmé's dice-throwing as a precursor for their assault on the hazards of quality, but they forget his cult of the old verse line. So much for the dance notations of free verse. The page and the screen assert geometrical frames whatever liberties are taken with straight-ahead linearity, the relentless progress from left to right, and all that justification according to the law of margins and the bottom line. But such fictions are relics of the cult of the old prose line.

The ends can no more ambush the means into new beginnings than the middle can massage its broken back. And despite the fascination with inventing rules to play with, language is not a game. The circular reasoning of poetic sequences provides a consoling exit strategy. What it loses in the recurrence of family resemblances it makes up for in the rewards of familiarity. While the great faiths invested in the poetry of number-crunching deserve the opprobrium of our latter-day priests, no-one has yet managed to write in such a way as to free us from the violence of metrical necessity. Language remains, however, the medium through which the speculative identity of logic and number reveals its antagonisms and its aftermaths. More is less. Against all the evidence that we won't stop believing in God until we stop believing in grammar, there's a lot to be said for the view that language knows more than it lets on, and loves nothing more than a good non sequitur amid the absurdity of surds. In the face of so many warring fractions, you could do worse than mutter sweet nothings and drop off to the music of infinite regress, and more often than not you do, you do your worst, before plunging into the full stop.

BLUEPRINTS & ZIGGURATS

STARKNESS FALLS

'This is a book just the way I don't like them:
scattered and with no architecture.'

                                   Stéphane Mallarmé

it will be
starkness falls
falling starkly
scorn in clover
to fretworking
the zine prose
dug duggier
the most dug
than wish rung
didn't ought to
see you shimmy
does as shimmy
is but starker

it will be
starkness falls
falling starkly
first stop mown
lawn to dishing
the dish as is
x is one that's
a real dishiness
turned tresses

it will be
starkness falls
falling starkly
the north car
park thisness
shame on each
and every went
analytical while
the grammar got
good got going
were all got off
and flamed the
night out starkly

it will be
starkness falls
falling starkly
uncouth parts
into the proofs
cue schematic
as dogma is
come again
the real lamb

the cartouche
turns achingly
beautiful say so
fall out starkness

it will be
starkness falls
falling starkly
over the drone
minded network
ooze south central
ash the clearings
star curst dudes
sew white hyphen
here and here and
stewing in trails
saying hit on that
time to the stark

it will be
starkness falls
falling starkly
laugh to pale
hard shoulders
where should
do glacial ire
paling scene
blazers are
as who purrs
then again
simply dated
and sewn stark

can but stupor
done to larks
the pall star
shot to starkness

it will be
starkness falls
falling starkly
bird to nail
smouldering
grant screeds
to stutter still
dew plaster
calls to cusp
embrasures
in which take
the taker falls
a felt starkness

it will be
starkness falls
falling starkly
one fell swoop
this is a case
of violations
the goth skip
shudderings
do nice detail
spar most of
the rest park
as the rest is
sheer starkness

PYLONS & PRYAMIDS

'It is
difficult
to know whether
the appearance of
the columns was responsible
for this word-play, or whether the
word-play determined the choice of capitals.'
Jean-Louis de Cenival, from *Egyptian Architecture*.

ridges
of tone work
reinforce concrete
stone against absolute mud
ruined capital in the brick shithouse
said pharaonic party back to slavery classes
continuously bound to sky rock the sun how narrow
courts become machines for dying in the pillars pink hewn
through flood planes tombs for myrrh and pylons on pillaged land
a grim staircase in shifts the necropolis of unsung labours upon a dead song

axes
of light pillars
best lend themselves
the palm the papyrus the lotus
colonnades in floral homonym a choice
plating on the facade column its fine white stone
giving representation to the sistrum plated golden cliché
how glitter sheds mystery then blunders into its slavish theatre
one more niche setting for finer face torus moulding and florid plurals
concave cornices ghosted by ribs of palm the beams down channels of flesh

timber
scaffold gone
no question of lebanese
cedar for stucco on workhouse
sans foreign aid rosewater compound
its migrant perfume expendable so cost cutting
corners off diagrams a blind door in limestone scars
pointing to exact hardness in the graphic roof of extraction
as all but mean structural weaknesses become mere archaeology
mark the desire for economy and its swiftest uses as the cheapest human

crown
tough matter
on such arched vaults
as four faces encompass news
their corners turning to the starry tent
rising from the resistance of the innermost room
into the central core of crudest lime shaven dead shell
until the final facing takes its dressed slab for the very night sky
the ratio of song to death giving forth palms over thumbs over waste
the slope spar spelt into the relative clause and dark trench of the nameless

BLUEPRINTS & ZIGGURATS

'whenever we find *architectural construction* elsewhere than in monuments, whether it be in physiognomy, dress, music, or painting, we can infer a prevailing taste for human or divine *authority*.'

Georges Bataille

'I have tried to put some poetry into the thing because we are going back to the source of civilization... The bridge and the cultural buildings, the art institute, the Garden of Eden, the cars are all absorbed into the scheme by way of the ziggurat.'

Frank Lloyd Wright on his plans for Baghdad

ambitious as Vitruvius to seem in pediment
torn to marks as sun unused to composition
burnt into loom writing as but a painful task
the measuring-rod far mightier than plaster
only its subjunctive construction done kin to
specs somewhat as a sigh in relief in shares
what divine intelligence and well laid lawns
its public build sawn into armour & gladioli
well versed in blued direction a mean optic
corona placed directly celebrant of women
carried into a slavery gluing eurhythmy into
Caryatid corpuscles a mark of the sculpted
rank married high the burden state holding
up in roof atonement so the enemies shiver
statues to shoulder hung to proper key how
blogging a genealogy of said proper gives
the eaves of skilled work being strike blow
course projectile in theatre a bronze vessel

placed in niches under seats for the actors　　hands
ears unable to encompass a theory sundial　　blued
harmony down to strain in tetrad and triad　　marks
the many as in artistic weapons that armed　　sever
make groundplan elevation as perspective　　brink

brick	earth	frame	works
burnt	water	mould	slave
spelt	rains	flows	chord
forth	slung	roots	brace

*

in	speed	what	but
the	is	matters	the
world	of	is	personal
of	the	not	moving
idea	wings	petrol	refined
much	obscurity	fables	predatory
bulges	that	burglar	charter
tallow	and	larded	hides
its	harbour	bliss	mills
spelt	plaster	volcanic	rock
spool	petal	off	blueprints
schemie	array	tuning	spikes
blue	blankets	singing	plunder
Dagon	sans	skeleton	constructs
folly	spread	spiral	diffusion
sonic	muddle	not	banal
vestibule	thinking	most	arch
prejudice	of	the	liberties
collations	sweeten	trenches	bungled
concrete	serves	ghetto	clearance
scuttled	rubble	starched	sewers

populace thus pressed below
stairs the carcasses drawn
and quarters crowned clutter

*

mass gables falling inwards
pinnacle still seen standing
fire the mines flaming
frightful high now obelisk
among the cream ruins
metaphor flayed balcony bars
sketches published blinded graphic
stock jobbers marching levees
that lake still draining
noble Doric butch playfair
citizen go box thyself
merchant cross city shambles
thistles at every corner
supplied with excellent springs
compact blue whin-rock basalt
beds quartzy sandstone smelts
porphyry passing into greenstone
embedded exhibits this trap-tuff
surface mamillary crystal crags
fierce crenellated teeth sprung
arabesques done into tiles
minarets or bigger domes
veins accessible by analogy
the falling water earthed
beached granite tumblers litter
scum supposed from dungeons

*

284

how villa leviathan
is carried away in
execution the bled
sprits were bursted
mains exposures a
way with the fairy
dentist's chair sky
criterion of gnomic
caressing his hand
spoke to shout the
colour of your car
are dark sides and
externals so mean
voice as colouring
be lake of that fire
subtle fluids of the
plebian beauty set
in democratic hues
and no slave other
to one of effusions
but much blooded
residence asterisk
boiling tritons and
nymphs even sand
blasting sung trash

*

a prospect of dentils carved to cornice an
entablature cushion gleaming bed esteem
for picture gallery in smart media sandpit
now soft now cool stole from marsh cut to
the walled apartment stating obvious pain
as ties made of charred olive or lately silk
no more but bowshot born a salient angle
rounded tower engaged to driving wedge

give teeth a saw say burnt brick mud and
the mighty law set into towers of the wind
marbling equinoctial gnomon inclinations
and left to blow the flanks her Hercules on
its circus for Venus sat in pride of harbour
overlooking peaks daubed in tawdry fires
oak shingle come thatched tuft crossbeam
scarcely referring to the ziggurat example
left in the wake of burning scars next thing
to refinement the bountiful timber yawning
deforestation ever more as the Easter isles
show how to triumph over a sustain pedal
the rock that passes all Ozymandian flares   trim
among the spoils of weathering though in   fire
baking sun justly named a builder's friend   mist
now tease out salt in chippy efflorescence   sunk

gush	drop	down	clay	hole
test	curl	poor	soil	sort
chin	spot	vein	seed	drop
look	clay	sand	wild	keep

*

fair	feeling	from	rules
ministry	to	certain	trains
beyond	stone	mortar	chimera
beside	pilasters	without	order
surmounted	monstrous	pepper	boxes
mock	fab	disgraced	kettles
stucco	the	super	sub
rods	splashed	in	ironing
for	verd-antique	the	wilds
mistaken	buttresses	holding	crockery
steel	in	the	floodplain
hymns	spelt	cursive	bricks

lionizing the construction worker
niche cottages for temples
woody dingle motion smoke
throng silver trunks corny
clusters along pegged thatch
wiggy mosses wandering lichen
and decay plain double
lattices flatly arched fluted
glory rusticated of mourning
the whole deep blue
melted away into sapphire
pale cities gleaming champaign

*

then spelt plaster volcanic powder mixes
lending strength set hard even on water
look to how slight a light tufa exfoliating
exposes the crumble to salt eating away
cannot stand a great heat but providing
more blush structural booty to placemat
for wattle and daub the more the worse
studs and girt all set to shrink once sunk
rot down courses settles and sags like a
dreary skin the spoke and human breast
to be furnished with open windows slash
sash for preference in the draft dexterity
hum general thrust merest counter palms
onto sheerest air all given up to asserted
maths so enthused by the asses and obol
what tongue to lash some guilty pleasing
decking out on top saying the pycnostyle
is an abomination cold intercolumniation
bring on the nonconformist spec to dusty
covers from a heavy shower eating into
diminished solids the shaft swollen ocular

laid under the brightest capital a column
and steps fit to wheel chair access ramps   asphalt
on pumice or sponge-stone funding body   abounds

honeycomb	ballistae	marble
scorpiones	tholepin	rubble
catapultae	triglyph	scree

*

one part constituting astragals overhung
rear porticoes perpendicular giving forth
the rule for the capitals sent abacus long
face of the volutes bleeding for warriors
the short shame let fall into the volumizer
big hair set to slay in metal head breeze
recalling the stonehenge spinal tap gripe
grooved into the projection of an echinus
bands of the cushions with axes aflaming
the back line stacks blasting microphonic
cod modules the gothic miasma here flies
screen scrapers touching up the red eyes
till over the frieze all monsters and dentil
seen plumb to reason in the fluted hi hats
lion heads purring into the grand reverb
set to boost a ring modulated resonance
unto Caesar seas of denim run to mud a
rock god module blazing the lyric stench
so curly ringlet dressed Dionysian bloom
to the golden axe under pyrotechnic sun
how the modal assemblage warps round
first phrygian then mixolydian and dorian   sunk
but slayers all to its free passage of note   stone
set to a plinth slash torus best left out rest   sinks

cymatium   wormery   brush
architrave   trochilus   reeds
acroteria   spreads   lava

*

caves   gray   coalition   grottoes
long   range   shivery   dazzle
snow   castellated   cresting   bunkers
done   for   cool   broken
mouldings   bow   strident   helipad
the   vibrations   shaking   Babylon
parking   lots   for   tanks
brick   dragons   scuttled   emerald
roof   cross   rafters   the
Moorish   arches   and   confused
conscripts   settled   in   rude
log   huts   unsquared   notches
vine   wild   in   valleys
ice   eternal   beneath   lasers
rough   brown   granular   surface
houseleek   moss   and   stonecrop
lowly   valley   for   torn
precipice   crest   crag   battlements
desecrate   the   Gothic   trefoil
ornament   rapturous   chimney   breasts
brightly   up   against   deep
Venetian   marble   staring   masses
sunny   glade   dewy   sward
always   surgy   oceanic   massy
green   and   elastic   vigour
spruce   or   natty   grotesque
desolation   of   sterile   peaks
Ausonia   thrilling   lozenge   borders

*

289

grub church news corp in hackistan
fleet street relocation union mashup
now marxism for avatars and disco
a white robe muse fraternity lay off
brogue nevertheless way to go says
comrade quip and wanton crank all
dimples sleek skips now frog justice
so leave the geese out of it Bacchus
down tools and tabrets this is silver
thrills kissing cymbals care of pearl
ridge all crisp inconstant done over
the four four goose steps in dérives
contra beaten box light on spoons
or what is it in the original Klingon
indices off the shoulder free breath
again as the numbers most exceed
clogs like feathers pumps like mills
burglar in penthouse phone hacks
how goes the hoedown on the dow
these days blue chip stocks reeling
now that's what I call redundancies

*

heard the grubbiest hacks of my class cohort
destroyed by soundbites dribbling Hegelese
blogospheres doing in focus group pollsters
segue to CIA flight Guantanamo connection
starring grief bracelets so tough on the truth
tough on the hollow-eyed cross-border strike
lips sawn in PFIs under the downtown Tigris
pigeon-holes passing amid research centres
the Hugh Grant eyes Murdoch-lite dossiers
crooning cash for arms for honours for the
terrorist brit pop combos shredding the air
the vats of plonk for millennium oh hot bush

city knees up Elizabeth Windsor where's yer
tupperware now some people's primadonna
goes hark the asbo vandal sing this is your
45 minute warning this is Ozymandias new
envoy scrubber with hand-offs for hand-outs
the longest sound bite ever to bite the hand   totem
that felt the shoulder that picked the winkle   oiling
that drowned the migrant worker that fled   pager
the commitment to redistribution this is your   smiler
45 minute briefing chin out to look feelingly   screen
two glossy thoughtless pegs doing the crony   casino
and the name is cheery blur, gloat of gloats   dome
look on my property portfolio and despair   prang

                              *

              balletomanes for class struggle
              well the sylph certainly marches
              on its stomach and great umbrage
              merely fuels an imagination test
              so to air all but the pet theory
              the three glowers cannot survive
              nor will suffice a will to foyer
              a lady in a very remarkable hat
              is fiercely partisan: avoirdupois
              and not poor music is the rough
              familiar with the gossip of the
              wings as breezes darn vandalism
              and of course brazen unnatural
              dancing is our proletarian art
              slyphides unite! sheer chrysalis
              awaits even a wooden counterpart
              wagging scarfs down ditto pipes
              panned to ecstatic matinée howls
              tarlatan realism in darts is so
              agreeable to the paper coquettes

so relative before the so saying
its collective is not an ornament
and everyone wilts into militancy
before the charms of fine raiment

*

for health care neat dice checking twists
texture for hotel retail semi-plain for the
office tight specs now construction crew
neo-industrialists in prog lime glad rags
leopard slipper shaker all heaviest raw
cometh the shredder cometh the beard
spandex a thrashtastic grunt retro-stonk
scuzzy perhaps into stray grunge sirens
alienation's alienation even self-induced
disneyland behind this ghosted context
the low-end sludge tripping out a mead
dirge as bland as the hairiest megaliths
and nothing to do with the question of
ornament or just gassy for Wittgenstein
a notion of pure architecture in threads
from shed to cathedral viz peasants the
mosh pit curious for façade as elevation
though the wall cast of local stones built
on no-one's bone those dwelling locally
and how else don't wish the walls down   head
to ashes for some foundation salon ruse   lung

posthardcore	spatialism	maquette
dactyl brick	gargoyle	faciatta
dogtooth	ball flower	foliage

*

no quarter in sky for capitalists and farmer
secure from robbery arching all composed
voussoirs even cutting slips figure luminous
herring bone patterns giving a burnt brick
frost and rime will pass by unhurt which by
ancients used vermilion sparingly as drugs
the malachite green purple Armenian blue
since spoke to lime proceed dug cinnabar
coats off Pontic wax shedding tear on tear
pound with a mortar chalk to madder root
equalled the leading ways for dirt control
security starts said entrance to the building
matting or carpet must be effective to part
soil and moisture from its coming footwear
traffic scars adequately sized to handle in
dot matrix features a heather colour sand
that and flowers of natron bound together
failing to observe such golden rules allows
offending matter to spread round premises
combining good looks and real functionals
to help mask soil available as tile or in roll
with thunderbolts the style carving creases
finial excluding base pyramid column dole
settle body load to position over dry room   security
concrete floor a most imported polish finish   cubical

crockets	pinnacles	soot
quicksilver	cymatium	pitch
edelweiss	corona	pine

*

long	shadows	of	cypress
blossom	the	glancing	aloes
pale	night	vision	statues
full	of	dashing	waters

distant
to
gray
embosomed
lances
moon
without
nothing
rod
but
lights
each
shelves
pinnacles
broad
proud
to
doggerel
baby
soft
houses
safes
sculleries
wherever
bonnet

precipices
mingle
tint
streaky
lie
surface
wings
but
dagger
more
by
brick
counters
of
shield
portals
electrify
doing
fortifications
votary
more
more
more
soil
castellated

taking
every
footnote
green
smooth
general
or
stables
of
laconic
channelled
stamped
clerks
the
crested
all
its
chalet
upon
of
than
than
than
breaks
zigzag

aim
opening
baroque
foliage
sward
Orestes
adjuncts
trenches
passion
avenue
mullions
Ur-hamlet
grocers
sugar-loaf
gryphon
risers
beholder
pagoda
bones
luxury
fortresses
keeps
dungeons
velvet
monotony

*

epithet
oriels
implosive
something
gods
thanks
however
massing

raw
project
interior
of
willing
to
back
bas-relief

tint
boldly
all
the
holiday
the
in
depicts

opaque
tendering
out
kind
inns
sanctions
Babylon
the

construction	and	all	ego
maison	individuelle	vast	glass
the	Dessau	spectacles	fouled
in	flimsy	software	shock
benign	tour	guide	joins
the	pillage	partition	frenzy
collar	embrasure	balcony	grave
voice	breeze	and	billow
will	shiver	as	looks
diorama	and	therefore	improper
snow	will	not	slip
the	Sumerian	ziggurat	look
this	side	scud	protection
Turkey	carpets	or	easy-chairs
cabbage	the	best	ivy
oak	too	stiff	putty-colour

*

the flower fadeth but the stems
become washing lines wrapped
in sediment & seaside simulacra
the shed to absent flourishing a
wall echoing wafts a blown trill
to the g string built on a topless
tortilla come bricks mortar and
drought cots from fishnet water
pink veils soiling in advert copy
over the picturesque turn round
Franco's army bosoms rampant
a rusting dome on the acropolis
as the local power ballad rocks
insects or mopeds pronouncing
surrealist tat and tache breezes
as Costa Live lets us in on which
dream in the archaic lava sport

red and ochre tiled roof picture
the grand bulldozers of tourism
c/o Deutsche Bank's passion to
perform their latter day Roman
circus upon purple scars vistas
worthy of Duchamp done froth
for the feat of egg & egg plant
eyeballs on choc stick pilasters
kiwi and lank linguini à la Dali
do the Bougainvilia poesi@rock

*

exilde for euer, bang to rights
   where pittie is fled and darknesse
bleeds books blossom crowded wills
   sion's stalls bound to graven stone
as aching wire does fencing threads
   round Ariel's fort and yankee hush

MERZ FAÇADE

'...a head-on confrontation with architecture is attended by underlying anthropomorphic connotations, i.e when "building façade" becomes "face", "window" becomes "eye", and "entrance" becomes "mouth". When we come face-to-façade, we recognize and experience frontality.'

Tom Porter, *Archispeak*

a lion protome
perched on top
of bank gothic
THE BIG A
Schwitters-ish assemblage
expanding towards Architektur
bits of newsprint   ur-column
formen im raum   -barn
leere im raum   -kiosk
MANIFEST PROLETKUNST
down the
Spitzweg
very act of building act fragmentation
new valleys
hollows   grottoes
catacombs
dance casino
deviant caves
doll housing

*

shoddy goods
qua monument
to the THIRD
international
bonk gawthic
autonomy tone
theses flaring
friendly fires
PYRAMID AND LABYRINTH
vietnam follies via korea   -park
press baghdad destruct   -skin
Luigi Moretti pasted into   -peak
watergate apartments or   -bark
the fascist fascia sports   -goth
SCAR LINEARITY
JUNTA NOSTRUM
down on the strip   gloss awning
vertical foyer   glassy firing
PASSERELLES
MEDIATIZATION
DATUM PLANES
double strip wave slab
SECTIONS
THROUGH
WAR ZONE
©APITAL YE$

*

gents polemical
dose scepticism
clerk bank goth
strangled mesh
YES-SIR URBAN TISSUE
helical   OCULUS
scorch   CRYSTAL
marks   BEACON
hadrian's rusticated fringe now showing
CREDIBILITY GAPS
VILLA dancing   club stuff
come Sun Space and Greenery
crown Gun Trace and Tuilerie
chrome Scum Grace Machinery
paste   PUREE
plate   GLASS
foyer   DRAIN

*

concrete grilled
cheese grate ark
dada vernacular
do gherkin condo
card board civvy
street face hood
yawns nun burka
shoe box shelter
warps grid trace
ferris wheelie bin
jabber eye chintz
skate park tracer
filing cabinet war
tent orange monk
egg crate lounge
I   II

*

299

O
SOLDIER DUCK
olde defamiliarization crows-nest
Ronchamp
a-frame   retro-fit
flies AVIAN   hand-stand
DOWN STAIRS LOO   SLAB
RENT   smoke stack   RENT
PERIOD   alley panda   SLOB
PORCH SKIN WASPS
slumming it in some style
manicured eyebrows showing near perfection
SURROUND   MOAT

*

jarred lawn transparencies
conical jammed in violent kin
cartouche balcony or stone
how they come to get porous
adapted to rusticate in buts
ambushed mid modillion sun
the lintel a tympanum round
pointy arches in such sorry
harbours turned colonnade
a loggia lining semidetached
_____

its love of clouds frescoes
smiling tondo bold Bacchus
doing the Lambeth jogger in
slip parking lot brown-field
binder for a bulbous codex
sconce of mags pavilions go
ducks in ubiquitous rocaille
rouched to within inch skirt
adding monochrome panacea
while loving the door so big

*

FACE HOUSE
huckster   adam
palladian   style
historicist steel toe caps
Mies in ironic swoons
the U-shaped
PIAZZA RES PUBLICA
paramilitary
ornament   head stocks
polycrime
guantanamo
shell suit stucco
c/o frozen spokes
the power-broker   blobs
AFTER AT&T   IN THE PINK
and frog marched kisser
inclusion zone

*

donut
DOME
cedar curves
this defensible closet
RAUM
THIS CELESTIAL SOFFIT
THIS REDUCTIVE FACTOR
THIS SWALLOWING SCOWL
THIS ZOOMORPHIC PROVINCE
fondle mint
torn U turn
when dark slates roll
OFF-AXIS URBAN WHISTLER
mannerist manna

*

shark BIENSEANCE
grilles and frills
nasdaq crawling all over alien labour
on homo erectus   marble
bunker-like slits   shades
plastic polymers   mouldy
BUNGALOIDS GET GO CHUNKY
NEO-VERNACULAR DRIBBLERS
HYPHENATION GONE AVUNCULAR

HIGGLEDY	A D	HODGE
PIGGLEDY	HOC	PODGE
DUPE CAP	WAD	SHAME
SLIPPAGE	SHY	SHEEN

POOL HALL
palazzo
pubblico
stitched up

*

RELIEF QUA BARN
blue bobble HUT
as per plastic assemblage
THE RAW   the raw
took him from streets
well lanes   well alleys
well shady ways   paths
gullies   tracks und lines
CUT-THROUGHS
up the blonde leaf arcade
up the back slurry passagen
ohne dabei minder abstrakt zu sein
RAW LIGHT   Kathedrale of bric und brac
erotisches elektrischen objets trouvées
sing lager strong bow p.o.w. stella
then cut a hole in the ceiling
give notice to the sleek timorous lodgers
HELLO DIY GROTTO FRENZY

zzzz zzzz zzzz

THE BRUISE THAT HEIDEGGER BUILT

'... in architecture it is the visible material, and spatial mass on which the inmost heart itself is so far as possible to be brought before contemplation. Given such a material, nothing is left to the artistic representation but to refuse the validity to the material and the massive in its purely material character and to interrupt it everywhere, break it up, and deprive it of its appearance of immediate coherence and independence.'

G. W. F. Hegel

hacker dwelling meniscus how go liquid   just
spans modular thrown open to open plan
no part in it nor no evolutionary prompts   as
that natural that rain yet ultimately social
will hold great matter of experimentation   love
then collective work in its own right how
united they stand the coop of landscape   collects
all easeful living to which spirit answers
are aspired said chain of endeavour skin   interiors
spar did it round the table a wood sickle
adventuress of native culture indigenous   become
and ever so modern fit with it landcapes
the post and beam construction here then   home
kitimat and kwakutl village (fig. 73) new
spine spire song dies an odd totem pole   shutting
the thing ranging playful to premonitory
the bruise that Heidegger built so tied up   every
set to pour concrete image or allotments
no kin or inhouse engineers according to   other
purred concrete slob edges expressed in
flamboyant canopy adding serene flairs   then
boasting to curved doubters to embrace
thus first ever plastic chairs on autoclave   shells
it's all happening or volume accentuated

to lozenge shapes ache to massing bulk   each
do dominion cities coining in definitions
mirage on parking penumbra as an only   finite
unanimous choice to go go electrification
to the blast it's all the same to yes amen   elevation
bastards torn through smooth talk medals
but so promoted into the sacred newness   hold
forced far up cry stark oh clean stocking
as markets proliferated so too modernism   shed
annuals donning bib & tucker and giving
it's hey ho slinging the beaux pants into   skin
a dust bag on on into over-bearing detail

stall city literally bound to margins slang
ltd. star if liberal attuned euros to scream   so
note in transatlantic moults to superbs the
geographic spray yields high proportions   arch
irregular & sloping building lot cum idiom
from west coast style to entrenchment how   its
genocidal mutiny an island of anglosaxon
field trips even after alienating suez crisis   fill
the fruit of the international go local flavor
all widening a whole field of architetcure   of
on climbing frames late of imperial hubris
landscape dense or lush and majestic barf   estates
till remarkably luminous grey light downs
a figure loot sublime profile of mountain   bitter
the hills that Hegel scorned till modernism
leaving slash bowl for a local poor ethos   grows
zip cuts and wound in very barked strain
a faded gasp of universal legitimacy hark   shifts
the grain elevator on oceangoing Empress
all without irony numen whiter than Ethiop   body
the perfection of efficients giving the evils
stream logged in kinds enslaving to techno   and

whereas the lyric fund growls design motif
spelt out diminished leaves respecting hush   soul
dainty but bluff geometer built in the USA
beaux part cum art deco craft predilictions   cutlery
as world war had run the yonk redundant
stucco upon stucco over the killing shelves   how
severs purity further evident in rendering
God the facade were to kill for so optimum   ideally
no fairy castle over a pointy headed peak
the bridge the shovel the briar pipe to bed   crashing
metonymy of pumice in the skirting boards
he want a machine to live in and less clutter   sounds
but still married to the earth works straying
for want of caryatid to cop off load bearing   flimsy

actually cramped in standardized quarters   firm
draped asbestos ranked statuesque in situ
its figurate living mind whose nature strolls   feet
within the floor area the budget will afford
pace Mayakovsky's pacing breath stretcher   then
atop a concrete slab laid upon minimalists
whose song of the box or cupboard draw   slippery
drives a coach and fiat through the whole
will to reside in architectonic vocabularies   tops
no bulky buffet arrangement needed here
later deployed in low brow configurations   nature
all hail Ikea and the stripped soul flooring
the cause economy in light brown parquet   makes
strung out vacantly over gypsum lego sets
till vermiculite sheathing holds each whole   no
of resin-bonded wood chips in rigid ranch
the blue-collar coffee set dreaming a buck   bounds
this is plywood world on the verge of MDF
a legacy of military design in every trainer   etc.
slash freedom's no blank indeterminateness

how goes it bonnie maid versatile linoleum   trenches
under which circumstances a double want
as a counter-poise to the absolute standing   puckered
partly too for something fixed and secure
feet up on the picture thinking homemaker   lips
while glamour steals a march on the bath
before sitting pretty up on executive foam   in
every picture window brought to you by
technology sanctified in modernist points   furrows
yonder the hum of happy wrecking crews
and the inherent problems of angular form   faces
giving way to the revenue view or upkeep
left to run from elegance to stark brutalism   come
hey you stop roaming in empty abstraction
keep your eyes open for lay Althusserians   physic
then there's the horizontal cadence calling

throttle squall so pulp sentiment pouring
scorning crisp to home of the year combo   drip
raised slab Miesian slotted into rocky crop
ample gives every bosom high rising utility   trickle
if residual neo-gothic articulate in masonry
was compact but glass block enjoying view   down
vista front cast concrete de l'esprit nouveau
as a model for inexpensive 'social' housing   harping
as if there's another kind you house banker
spreading parks in euphuistical clerestory   scam
only the best for patio sets glazed gloomily
into middling distances where poor folk go   how
amid wheely bins spanking tame angularity
turn up cape cod retro styling to historicos   beds
set for cheerful living what is pulls tongue
the reflex gag in sheer concrete weeping   backs
mourns charm suffused torture up and up
pick the wage scope demanding finer stock   rifts

306

and above all the tree and columnar spray
showering acanthus over bushy carpet and   middling
bring me the head of estate management on
a plate and talk of sad suits in Bloomsbury   even
it comes out on wasp bombers c/o Boeing
apparently limitless cheap gaz in structural   your
minimalism it will do many rivers to syphon
the feral report source taking hard headed   extended
low rise pokey do the multiflex said to be
the holy grill of prototypical cheap guilded   limb
before burnt professional saturation smarm
forcefully yet amicably like staid intellects   for
shuffling up through the mollusc categorical
as talk of creative energies leaves the room   family
spinning in concealed mirth the gauche do
sparks trend drainage from growing spots   kids
tangle torn the elite corps looks down upon
hovel dance set baking a black polo sweat   car

        the bond's as secure though
        effected by different means
        for said family on a streeper
        site a tricellular stressed-skin
        elliptically vaulted building
        conceptual variations further
            disposed
            among   spills
            eating
            bathing   staining
            and
            sleeping   loved
            with
            grades   parts
            nesting
            existing   well

owner
occupied   broken
foliage
breathing   parts
steely
larks   such
gridpark
frames   that
snoozing
through   sinking
winding
wires   pulls
settling
into the raised slab solution
in admittedly flatter locution
intent in their no less purist
pavilions of instinctive glory
urging lyricism over rations

boxy-wood frame and concrete
ranged around a modesty pack
lately doubled in upon circulars
for the more angular deep cave
pitching a mythic dog or domus
including a special custom fitting
  graphite
  down   heart
  vellum
  textured   spanner
  where
  plains   fittings
  depend
  stimuli   buckled
  expanded
  volume   down

therefore
moody   among
respect
naturally   cuttings
setting
sublime   frosting
northern
environs   each
broads
bricking   killer
artificial
fireplace   cabinet
focals
the cross-axial kitchen in liquid
plane form volume and facture
showering the polygonal drones
and arcs around a central pool
the texture to the exposed wing

the house of ideas is life as lived
use what is there to lend meaning
and memo to blend varnish cedar
a building should celebrate a site
its should as divine functionalism
disturbs the natural to a minimum
    scoops
    affordable   light
    imaginary
    bank   facing
    managers
    expendable   streams
    livings
    reflecting   flexed
    pooled
    strands   along

ruthlessly
screened   industrial
from
intellectual   cartilege
fabric
therewith   such
proletarian
golfers   privacy
televised
declining   priced
locals
while   to
fieldstone
hearth   die
roasts
colored   for
wallpaper
growth spoke of as western scene
for people not for plants creatures
until sold on the golf course circus
sing climate milieu technics encore
once more puppet imaginary client

but warned of looming urbanicide
the trend embraces half measures
dunked in pure opportunism slurp
ironically barely captures the half
acceptable face of countless crazy
stone dykes in Inca parody stacks
spaced
between   prefab
living
then   does
sleeping
spaced   screen

between
structuring   the
material
projecting   work
concrete
modernism   life
through
class   simples
dividers
tongue   your
and
groove   glass
sharing
laterals   half
bordering
upon   full
sterility

a gambit reflecting military gear
marshalled among said enfilade
to spatial freedom where dusting
the reliable barometer of public
sky bungalow such unlikely term
being the wood generated vistas

cognitive architecture involves the prop in   notes
stays low mental skeletons that don't vary
to those most sceptical of its representation   screwed
suck in the causal draft buttressing events
otherwise done municipal verily maecenas   to
cometh the pool and cabaña oer the hydro
as starry fire takes a collegiate gothic look   skirts
giving curtains of glass the once standing
pool of lit ennui throwing up the exposed   choked
beam overhanging eave shingle pitch roof
laughably called for genuine regionalism   linen

here plagiarists roam over the old carcase
rather than patch up a mouldy design tort   analogy
bleat bleat comes the all new humanismus
enamelled till the flush bridles to scholarly   masker
decline one time capitalism all but killed
architecture as a decent profession herald   are
tide tilted into breeze block import domes
talks up ¥€$ down neo-modernismus way   joys
head in hand to face the built environment
simmers over ground once marked to clear   in
be concrete dressed in concrete universals
with Prada conduits well pure Tudorbethan   all
while surfer epistemology frankly panders
you propose simply to drive into the night   the
down ghosted script as yer man nearly did
the house strives to open cities within a city   rooms
leaving space junk where the heart was just
a divorce from context to gather its grooms   sifted
en route to Janus or the Jamesonian glossy
the epithet trade playing a blinder or news   through
how the ear is space junk in petrol cat suits
that's Devo redux or elephantiasis in Lagos   in
all colonial animus ready on veranda decks
did someone lose a plot on that built fiction   waking
well nevermind let's hear it for scarlet litter

different to the style to begin by levelling
trees the living tree surely as a fire break   play
incorporated into lives as if they had been
bulldozed cedar turning off the water table   areas
tank flowering club toe on autodidact pram
earmark the million then go a-slum clearing   break
dinky & sparky serves the full slate bustling
doing what cash can't how evensong fade   frowns
rips to cherry blossom here's ville radieuse

if you could but lash the wood from forests   down
of symbol amid how the large sun balcony
gives forth from tree-screened moonscapes   ramp
pilotis of type B over stencilled graveyards
worth rich natural sluices and panic button   lit
the social climate becoming the more social
every living room in birdsong to waffle cork   fords
sacked on blue oxymoron of social housing
roof for laundry and recreation giving a lie   fit
called outside space as if there is cut space
slash again do unit aluminum brush strokes   for
lions over the gate bent to carry favourites
when the Spartans call asking for protection   the
before everything's synonymous with lowly
income ghettos how that fell off borghetto   usual
to jerry-built plaster over the displacements
spy the Corbusian trinity of light air & space   stress
fields and the surest index to chard gibbet
option prefab tucked up in reflex low costs   woods
repeater sick flowering phased fenestration
allude if you can to surgical precision plenty   build
plywood panel and acoustics bless linoleum
blunted in a hospital vista all done inside in   the
principles on light truss to excessive bends
but every effort spent to escape institutional   budding
even fresh man psych all tomorrow nursery
it's a final bleak tuning in greeting concrete   boy

the concession to civic dignitas was mainly   how
structural pillars bringing on the marboleum
tiled washrooms improve classroom access   pink
with stylism absorbed in the loss of function
the concrete of that philosophy said lovely   glimpse
by a thousand pans but lacking whimsicals
at least new tech school does ultra-modern   derives

that electrifying lucidity when budgets rise
up the sawtooth roof windier than eyes on   flesh
spoon fodder for said taxpaying plutocrat
keen to spanner in an industrial-arts facility   from
taking the oath amid the pilastrate so clear
so forever renounce imitation Gothic rump   wraps
the uplift that is iconic dismal turned sunny
not a mere carpenter pumping out palazzi   stained
all hail signor Brunelleschi of the numerals
how Quinque Columnarum etc bent rules   fiery
working up the bill of quantities and rights
that the territory of disegno expands each   dues
field op see Palladio delineated for proles
sundry vitrifying agents of winged cherub   from
marching on the capitol via lavatory/stacks
bring down spry tyranny of sleek numbers   window
so visual qualities suppress formal rigours
slab climbed an L-plan office high rise yes   grace
it said yes to the dance of human portions
blown on the days of the marble stairwell   rippling
skip to the startling tartan of metal mullion
and transom filled with gleaming opacities   even
one more jalousie to ferment the evenings
not so much conserved as bastardized for   thrown
commercial tenants like there's any other
expressive universality of abstraction jams   spent
enhanced by light shining plexiglass panel
how factory sash forms clerestories of moon   even
accommodating iconoclasm to late dogma

an apse in some belvedere off outer space
the cat brings in architectures of the visible   exiled
a bowl bending mother's milk and the give
its thing coming on global so roundly spied   from
occular proofs viz tuning typos giving head

show forth the campanile the harsh cyclops   its
of the lens bending the bar cone to chevron
calling A-frames to a temple of baby bonds   idea
sewing Abraham's tent over Factrolite glass
the residence was all silence all portals shut   palace
and the pillars built of white stone via plastic
don't talk of bi-nuclear planning or suchlike   handles
rapt at the dominion from built-in cupboards
new stakes in the land radiating under-heat   breathe
esp. in the domestic field like there's another
pure yet lyrical pavilions shudder it timbers   nymphs
now demolished by sticks of fresh tamarisk
as a measurer of heaps despoils even steers   and
as the tongue is some kind of plummet helm
tales of each Sinuhe with livings and utilities   number
shake out the monocline roofing as symbols
do the butterfly settled on a leaf hype poem   shower
taking up the slacker trend hereabouts close
so close it reflected the average disposables   curtains
amid ongoing close supervision in daytime
a tricellular stressed-skin elliptically vaulted   give
lift-slab solutions as cute as an Adam ceiling
showering the client in orthographic project   moulds
the project of which Being spoke so harshly
where real woodland gives forth satyrs still   dating
download brochure to scribe off blue data
schooled in the idea of two axes and recall   give
the architect in most post-Renaissance offices
defined precisely in opposition to its intimate   bold
involvement in the onsite construction process
freeing something from someone signed sky   ruins

EMBRASURES

here an almshouse there
a palladian disability unit
baldachino for ciborium
and embrasures of within

angular		lean to
capital		roofing
bloods	care	single
capital	shed	roofing
block	tree	screen
capital	folly	framed
cushion		rip offs
capital		scallop

old style scandal mews
in debt to public private
injection traceries swag
now a pension torus in
wall to wall vernaculars

CUSHION CAPITAL: a cubical capital, also block capital, sculpted to suggest a cushion weighed down by its entablature. A name given to Romanesque church capitals cut away on four sides leaving vertical faces. Bank vernacular for the buffer of liquid assets set off against the haircut value of securities at risk of delay in the realisation of liabilities.

limit slate loading blurs
into cross section beams
harming a tense strainer
over primed pragmatics

concrete		bonded
tendons		concrete
serving		fissure
fatigue	sleep	papers
scheme	sweet	finished
striking	stress	untold
buckled	curve	labour
tenders		untold

with it elasiticity ranges
revolt to reinforcements
to brute grout the stress
and pile cap for footing
its frames are not linear

MONOLITHIC ROCK: a confusion of singular stone monuments with built or natural features, or with monotonous heavy rock groupings. Cf. 'A reinforced concrete structure is a combination of beams, columns, slabs and walls, rigidly connected together to form a monolithic frame. Each individual member must be capable of resisting the forces acting on it...' Mosley, Bungey & Hulse, *Reinforced Concrete Design*.

minus tools at the going
rates plus incidentals to
the tune of plant to the
interest of spent capital

excavate		trimming
loam sun		of layers
clay dung	ads	ditto mud
chalk rock	scar	tempering
throwings	each	puddling
by shovel	tool	clay turf
removing	face	stackings
levellings		wheeling

labour constants as due
per cent then reckoned
upon reduced efficiency
in output as compared
to pre-war calculations

CONSTANTS OF LABOUR: an abstraction figment to average out-turns extracted from labour, and so a ready reckoner ignoring nature, size, situation: 'The vertical transport of earth has been found by experiment to equal 24 times the labour of moving the same distance on a horizontal plane when barrows are used, and 14 times when horses and carts are used.' *Hurst's Architectural Surveyors' Hand Book* (1932).

labour opening to wood
work often adds on half
more labour but straight
double for head of door

jambs &		framed
soffits &	sunk	square
wrought	work	the flat
rebated	done	denials
grooved		backed
included		per foot
plugs &c		roughed
tongued		edgings

add if herring-boned or
solid at the back if hung
folding add if each face
bead flushes extra butts
giving this ditto veneers

GEOMETRICAL FALLACY: a disorder associated with delight in concrete reinforcements and left right justification. The confusion of tidiness with beauty calls forth geometrical negation even from lovers of grids: 'It would seem that the tree is an element essential to our comfort, and its presence in the city is a sort of caress, a kindly thing in the midst of our severe creations.' Le Corbusier, *The City of Tomorrow.*

Jerusalem stone as the
jokers annexe greater
their belt of built fabric
cladding the collective
memory as occupation

urban		stone
shack	hilltop	bylaw
roused	phone	newly
shame	masts	merely
colony	sticks	dressed
drying	stones	stick-on
amber	dishes	colonial
yellow		veneer

dishonesty to material
as its build emblazons
the sign of the intifada
graffiti engravings the
make up now petrified

BEDROCK: a monumental muddle, in our most unnatural history, of metaphorical essence
with appearance: 'the very material used for cladding the expanding Jewish Jerusalem has
become one of the most important branches of the Palestinian economy, quarried mainly
from the bedrock around Hebron and Ramallah...' Weizman, *Hollow Land*.

jungle seeds house
the ending expanse
precincts as raised
sunken square toe
cone pyramid eyes
each sky to dome

from the armchair
flattened pedestals
put to bald counts
they have piled up
soils and the soiled
still bruising of sea

baby faced jaguar
fled from tourism
each or then some
well spoken niche
so passes the clad
and squalid motif

harm fret patterns
taken for the gilts
the flanks bristled
daily life such as
methods for skull
flattening the child

so called acropolis
reminiscent of the
name most of all

rope stone binding
imitates the bulge
of an earlier wood
form over in grille
a snail observatory
the serpent header

palisade in waters
the false arch held
amid its vegetation
and the temple of
inscriptions tuned
to human sacrifice

amid the low land
of hills sunk pools
lend water cisterns
a plumage in stone
before petrification
takes off in biscuit

stone masks well
almost everything
culled into facade
each dressed brick
from water canopy
to deserted capital

rarely this military
starring event dogs
slopes corporation

in the burnt seed
down used quartz
kept dogs or bolt
no more but slow
its obsidian arrow
all for the trading

moon pyramid all
added stucco mud
the missing temple
dubious room idol
as pilaster warriors
so sweetly to wind

bas-relief of eagle
swallowing hearts
one half removed
the flesh workers
can labour dry can
fire snakes breathe

skull rack still flu
in the war cabinet
park figurines due
south low writhing
in the boring navel
and butterfly scarf

then a wild horde
the make crusher
pilasters sacrifice

the stumps slaved
stelae in dots and
dashes zero shells

that and ritual kills
the brilliant frieze
maths to astroturf

bag simple blood
the copal swallow
bled city to rushes

what's the Mayan
for quick property
flutters giving the
coat plaster swish
really a city of the
dead and the fiver

they came by foot
and left in camera
bridge sunk below
the sea the greens
the stubble and in
wild horses friend

skeleton removed
for further cutting
remarks like their
academy from the
ashes scurf debris
by monolith glue

the style goes hand
in hand with dialect
church as instance
balustrade frenzy
before mass killing
squat flower cells

clear stripe dating
elaborate coiffure
the clay figurines
to crow fiery calf
coming up rosiest
of the rosey burns

distant precipice
sparks from land
of black and red
heart burn crane
the blood thirsty
no they did drink

MINE OWNE IS BUT A HEAP

'in a majority of cases the ruined buildings became the quarries for
their several neighbourhoods, and the portions that remain to us
were spared only because the supply of material was greater than the
demand for it.'
          Butler, *Scotland's Ruined Abbeys*

of welcome ruins to stand
as broken as present use
in the charm note edifice
romanesque school parts
cut to dogtooth demands
while velvet carpet lawns

feeble & fondly garrulous
girl about in eddied tides
a sombre barge bearing
internments for wild isles
laid waste by said horde
and invading modernists
brutalists sacking rubble

onward heathen darkly
smarting as to bricks or
stony soils of later irony
spent surmising simples
that hills rise to ethereal
lamby landscapes each
cloud purple crag peaks
curious mail a clad slab
to banded capitals crude
and far from symmetrical
the death of geometry as
most welcome relief from
the picturesque elements

as yes go suck transept
the good is not to choir
its so slender colonettes
not a poorest part being
there suck the sarcophagi
flocks blessed in tourism
that vies with the capital
fluting to cushions under
marble filled with fossils
how as a constant drain
its floodlit resource sump
gives way to ribs a dark
tone to the scorched pile

COLONNADE

purpling parts
participles stop
no not paragon
knows the cuts
that other cuts
prefer to should
as to showboat
the muscle lags
hot cash is hot
ripe fees is all
at the point of
simple sciences
situationism for
giving it crème
tangled scanner
a ruse warbling
the idiot roomer
yow to drizzle
we be the strike
committee can

line the corpse
for dead labour
the sheen tome
boot camp for
girls so rrotic
as to strip paint
off the double
yellows how the
days turn pink
is dusted onyx

cable carpets
bomb quilted
that that stench
be applied for
funding the slip
dune here soap
oil thing to shift
and then reek
will be heavies
soup tooth ray
while the tort
just diffidence
this in a same
dance factory
whatever else
there's affect
suppression no
blood on sheer
slip dot ramble
part lie part sic

parts lark spent
push ahs come
after it dawns
the blown lame
blurring scams
as the end here
nigh on drawn
blaeberry is but
a thing hardly
ever seen ever

maybe not clipt
diacritical cries
given to comma
virgules in drifts
of parenthetical
pathos as lucid
punctual yawn
births the cold
some but salve
in conclusion
stop mr postman
enough gives
a focal shifter
blames the how
long have we
got sepia swaps
sans serif spine
to stoop spleen
labour lawns
plume stones

and then just
rank belletristic
better part of
gurred reserve
cumulus screed
clod of the urb
but wait it is
a drone media
say unobtanium
rust belts off

a red top look
class levitation
for middle-class
kids trying to
sound hard so
the pluck make
surfing a sicky
muddling middle
the very melody
as the sold gram

folded into font
dogma to glyph
not for negation
a middle voice
to obsolescence
said the sapphic
to the queasy
lapping blurred
how go dozing
parks the grime

pool for peas
freezer bags
blur into spot
dusty & sparse
glottals ahead
in abstractions
the struggle to
take in typecast
cloud classing
that but clouds

SPANDRELS

the spandrels go dark
but not in any rushes
then not quite warmth
more draining scarred
and some guest studio
some greatness flames
thinking a lived cage
and a bussed argument
takes to colour glass
where old house dries
a mould comes through
and these lack filler
lack any hidden depth

the spandrels go dark
from want of a better
way of holding to sky
to the shared horizon
to each place held in
atmospheric pressures
there comes the scale
and its heaviest hand
is the trumpet piping
a demise of classical
class politics a song
whose darkening clock
goes reify reify this

the spandrels go dark
spelling archest cups
pretty rich gargoyles
and darned fiction to
suit some maker meets
one with light browns
and all my very thing

the spandrels go dark
and the quality darks
are a season mourning
the fall as autumnals
do the rounds the new
black fades off sable
stone does strokes in

doing scandal skips a
neck dimed to strange
the impacts limed the
phrase larks searched
once pursed screaming
now roof felt or sky

the spandrels go dark
destructions still to
come and agony blends
labouring for a fifty
per cent haircut debt
rescheduling in fiery
doubting a pure build
gives regimes of seem
a transitional castle
object in the temples
of terrorism as marks
show bullets here and
here cue losing looks

the spandrels go dark
as the bridged reason
takes turns for worse
shows in spent detail
how to fact structure
into sheer moment sag
the sadness the light
potential to concrete
one universal after a
friend of said praxis
and another friend in
talks with the church
for want of a shelter

any direction any but
resistance prevailing
how to sever its arch
capitulation to pitch
the throw of the loam
on propped up leaders

the spandrels go dark
just as the clocks go
back and back a night
that oblivions forget
only to bake for dawn
bricks to mirror soul
upon carbon firmwares
sepia come tree rings
that narrative cracks
what animus retaining
spirit in the dresser
and some damned irony
for conceptual mortar

the spandrels go dark
then brighten up from
the perspective their
revolution sheds over
impending social moss
that as a leaf patina
ferns catching in mid
sentence its bindings
shirked down to birds
a sick building drift
blown into a friendly
fire drill who clears
the desk and corridor

SKYLON SONG

o
sky
song
skylon
half way
house and
paths lost but
summit meagre
brick charred ruin
burning burning so
still the none comes
and portals to watery
beds how sweet flows
concrete steel a thread
its once and future city
shows this slender cigar
steel that floats and flags
bonfire of the modernists
how each visible support
does a lash propaganda
sleek symmetry as cakes
for the millions who saw
who came who felt a sky
high into vertical breeze
to scrap of ashtrays and
satellite dishes air spear
here over the whimsy of
fabric and braced bulbs
their aluminium lattice of
something darkly atomic
who gave us the housing
scheme as advertisement
such as its fallen to furies

its towers and gates and
walled antithesis to each
point of consumption the
framing the gilded dome
in nursery screen colour
what is fondly fed out as
with a few trees for foils
skirmishes against pains
curtains to slender spars
all windy a most useless
art but drawn ever in to
dissed city a warehouse
and mobiles in smashed
vermilion this if the fires
were what we give and
giving take for the walls
each charter'd dressing
so onward goes the bid
that tenders to the tune
of can we fix it and yes
we propose a lingering
among ruins still for no
of all that boldness still
will so bear its deadest
scribe by whose means
the city will be opened
and the skylon well that
hang up a bit in the air
held astonish the place
dreaming a toyshop for
an eternal disaster flick
then on in flat pack life
cul-de-sacs a vernacular
throttled birth ever new
riverside property scam
buildings are not boxes

with four walls and a lid
said Vergil to his Dante
come in from off streets
where thinness is made
blueprints for new town
sensible or not too dear
practical but rather dull
but at least a trend from
away to gloom of wars
who have not shelter no
great gusts of socialism
guided by is it a moon
you call the anchor or
late symbolist smudges
there where its shades
are wholly covered up
olympiads harsh in the
citadels of the east the
brack of building dust
hosed down in lottery
funded circuses but a
low noise circling still
here the margins are
just margins or more
screed huddles about
its person and directs
towards a city arising
and best left for quiet
singing behold dissed
city behold the police
manner a brokenness
playing the part as of
Brutus the republican
its frozen crust off the
festival hall set into a
frenzy of mezzanines

its much vaunted sky
for the shy abyss of
property prices the
still fighting stars a
noise of business
till the artificial
is least serious
almost dance
airs turning
as rational
to stay up
amid late
showers
and let
lights
left
lit

THE VIEW FROM ROYSTON CAVE

hacks in solidarity how Royston cave worms
are low sound drones over the blogged news
how spiritual debris rends to old carapace
the curse of the conservationist so cometh
doing good until chemistry set speculation
does a laying on of trowel oh templar crud
shifts in grotto crypt on chalked up skies
filtered evening set too for the god squad
and associated grammarians setting fire to
feigned duping capes hewn to warrior monks
thence but soft to wan how the acquisition
gives up every cheque to a faked etymology

scourge of grammarbot to   here
tenders infinitive hacks
off forces the addressee   were
set to please attachment
here flume burns spammer   worm

shot to grumble stepping   spun
grammar checked software
item: termite trawl over   soft
sandal targe band coving
preceding to verb modify   bits

sing far too many people   that
as smilingly hack bounce
post a not trespass sign   chew
to name teeth come bloat
is that a copyright weep   cave

between the hour the dot   idol
user envelope pager they
have rights and will bot   blog
to bot user to page edit
as in the tone plate mod   song

spend the darkness lightly, spend darkling
light in the gripe how else survive quiets
so much for this dark boost all cult grail
dowser so much for gloved crusading butter
which cannot but be laid strange and hired
out among guilts down Icknield Way plunder
spores, the very scurfs pave soul leverage
as will be bold to the squalid strain will
be squalid to the colder lux will be scald
firmament then to more pumice tenders, cue
the local history swat team and no mistake
that said none sicker does terminal prayer

laziness kills insert no   slow
jane gland can do figure
just turn this thing off   down
across the autotag preen
carp lock update metatag   this

a sock puppet to sans ad   fine
source turn sceptic feed
all ditto to quiff creep   noun
in bare core filter funk
as said bot policy sadly   hard

attach key flames dismay   done
sprinklers on hand lunch
spleen item: in new edit   none
reel buffet to armed you
continue to receive font   turn

sets but no longer bliss   away
on fire to variety reels
perceived stress provide   this
a paradigm sponge mixing
yes kills to affect list   much

in the esoteric cave of their late showing
idols it is back to the octagon mimic dome
of the rock of the grail of the electrical
new age once upon an omphalos before heart
bliss meets and dying how a bottle hollows
out to prose in a thick of the uninhabited
time a conquest so spelt grot dissolutions
in her final sepultre as the work is broke
a cut say researchers that smacks of small
art as the figure with drawn sword in hand
is suborned to represent an arms franchise
that speaks to the combed taste of the age

genre boys copping bleed   note
the going rogue junk spa
that material in literal   duly
bruises tango ditty duly
for best practice a wrap   sent

you selected for despair   pine
in filling in the online
application song under a   back
data partner to unmoving
click remove me now that   well

hummed spool item: spoon   lame
tune a water cooler down
in pragmatism central as   door
good seed how does fluid
bounce stacks in beatnik   pith

the rolling neck sweater   gone
a pixel doll just double
glazing let how a satire   then
dayglow need to know the
lie while we connect you   some

unassisted by the passage to darker colour
marks of cremation, marks of wailing dough
a rude iron gouge, with bustle among large
quantities of animal bone and blunted nail
a carpet in tracing back to Temple village
Rosslyn house of the risen film franchises
production costs skimmed off each buy back
how I am come back filing worm pulp rushes
and grains, flee what kills or pains, note
said chalice as venom's industrial tourism
shows good report, how the worm passes for
news just in here's to all joy of the worm

dear all to seminal bell   line
glance today as a series
slides followed by draws   grid
server footprints always
no missive bloom at fall   does

given current wince sigh   dirt
be nominate not attended
winging the name zillion   type
a perl script for losses
read loses for suit case   font

for bully read breadline   from
for brat read amuck sewn
duplicity in lot motorik   pale
to dark showing it crown
a farm less likely dance   pulp

if but can not read this   with
please refresh to browse
brow gone click unlike a   less
lease to creamier trials
scoops but name sure and   care

Mahood to Worm, Mahood to Worm how can you
spell the grace of sunken gnostic graffiti
with chalk down of animal and found matter
can you read me, you are in present danger
of death by pedestrian commas off bloggers
grown so fashionable that it's open season
on the idle carpet of honeycomb appearance
where spent candles are mistaken for signs
in emergent deterioration as a spare parts
chapter slaps its preservation orders over
the most promising dust in all Christendom
and would save anything from organic decay

nude engine dimples this   part
metric item: down filter
a ruse twine lock in zip   rips
data tuning partisanship
are all holds about held   then

about a dread side skirt   rose
summary in do thing cape
gracing your advances in   tone
parts long the hurt film
showing when boots a rag   rows

nick tones show to where   fell
read were cold read pale
for wretched do wreathed   down
here are further designs
to after party ampersand   sore

in dark blue variant ire   from
keen corporate shed bean
chord trenches turquoise   live
zing the way gives to up
up strong the second lag   loss

now gives up another transparent worm that
has been identified as one for the biocide
as a kindness will kill off the host agent
set to our old friend lack of funds a.k.a.
meagre scraps off the cookie cutter sharks
and though the cave entertains much carbon
dioxide from an all singing motor industry
how threatening gas burns will to metaphor
out of all proportion with a history paved
over the skeletons of lost hardware glyphs
suggesting an underground tube map for the
holy land with post hole sanctions to boot

inflammatory flexes that   host
x and y that wrote of an
open accession a pivotal   cost
on model they also serve
to iced din lung in info   cool

now at this page bounced   arms
links from a more carbon
hungry site referral for   shed
ethics read solar glazed
or worse item: solid ban   told

on punctuation litter as   data
if a doubt click logo to
each to delete do button   sets
marks mistake mile drive
torts in sundry omission   with

kind not liable soft sud   cold
by way of kudos even off
set to otherwise threats   call
energy storm prepare for
brownouts keep hard copy   dirt

but still as in some unremarkable geometry
points to a prison jar best left unsung or
carvings turn upon unremembering crusaders
once set on bringing grammar to their mass
their gold filling for readily dug bunkers
and burial plaque embossing every pickling
of chalk how the clean slate or spread bet
conclusion shows checked software triumphs
a river spent tooling up for better denial
while the motion is to encircle gloss camp
fantastic so spammed from the chalk-eating
worm comrades set up with soft furnishings

copy cough uses bot comb   scud
pine of dulness infinite
in lines note who courts   mist
a daftly v deft just the
if clause needs spawning   dues

cares unreal grammar cop   term
saying nothing about the
substantive as deference   uses
dark question to assault
previous form as profits   once

workers who neuter grass   puce
roots in sympathy scarce
to injure participle bot   then
click here to be victims
shine outage set to bore   told

there is no period ditto   over
grammar punk burn a self
styled vigilante against   best
typos in some defacing a
more than sixty year old   felt

set fire are the killing fields down drift
of open-cast seams, brown-field demolition
meanwhile a conservative estimate gives up
150,000 deaths a year said to be linked to
industrial air as epidemiology by postcode
passes off the blame onto sorry dust mites
despite pertussis vaccines seeded to raise
immunoglobulins all while mercury exposure
goes among waste burns chimneys crematoria
heavy metals worming their way through the
blood stream down DNA transfers into lymph
maps of lung flow here comes dark fibrosis

moral fibre apostrophize   said
as in on story continues
to even slightly spanner   down
next stop burning zipper
field fill feel to noise   then

jump cuts well well they   dust
hatch some of these user
be small pets and babies   rugs
in access to solids copy
to run over the language   zoom

the shape spark gives in   into
tense assassin metaphors
abandoned how evident or   quip
just a potion suffix top
witnesses in spoke barks   plus

item tremble in plangent   well
parabasis frontal boughs
given to apple the apple   some
most fitting because the
rotation facsimile blows   boom

said chimney smoke stacks stack up masonic
rites but not for comrade worm so drowning
in rotten research what with an alarm call
thanks to acid rain, pesticides then again
down wind of the Pembrokeshire oil complex
the highest breast cancer incidence in the
industrial world, while essential minerals
in UK vegetables fall reported down by 75%
before the cocktail of our daily emissions
gives nickel vanadium cadmium lead mercury
acidic carbon to name how one grammar goes
to ground this anechoic inhalation chamber

stimulus arrows to chest   skip
after long look at novel
found attune to schedule   that
a burst mains shown tiny
took back to the brutals   call

even though the findings   into
suggest aspect fragile a
piece petty tender while   dead
fast shaping their peaks
turn to buts one pockets   sets

assigned a gender such a   hack
claims farming the gloom
like German as more like   hewn
who bore the bits caller
as some poverty turns to   saws

tense press tent strands   bled
the lead study author so
print friendly once pose   from
the quick how in grammar
we trust takes to grotto   lime

EQUIPOLLENCE

the cost of this text
          is living beyond its means

the cost of this text
          will be beyond even the fuzz box neuter stop in parquet
          blooms

the cost of this text
          is giving it the mop floral the glove glitter the constructivist
          turn to text as a material relation friend even passing
          through through too the relative and not the preposition
          beyond which evens can be willed can become a will

the cost of this text
          will not be charged to your account save as alms for
          oblivion next stop sins of omission period then spent as
          some residual of family of kids of kidders of kind of you

the cost of this text
          is ready to face up to the futures market but is so set against
          filling holes in its public private finance initiatives with
          grammatical compromises c/o ruled resemblances

the cost of this text
          is torn from the living daylights of the call for bedtime
          stories for hugs for references for letters of recommendation
          for marking for cleaning for the love of living of doing of
          being of anything but this now as this now

the cost of this text
          will not be televised

the cost of this text

　　　is limelight over lumpfish over leggings over eggs over easy
　　　like highdays and holidays over a dance of rest not rested
　　　but over it so over it so over the afters

the cost of this text

　　　is a fraction of the sums spent paying other people to do
　　　the dirty to do the cleaning to do the childcare to look after
　　　the young the sick the infirm the not quite with it or just
　　　those who can ill afford the time off from instrumentality
　　　to sharpen their lyric mulch into something resembling
　　　potlach come res publica

the cost of this text

　　　is careering into networks of the unmentionable in pursuit
　　　of have you considered yourself as this unit as mental labour
　　　as this having impact

the cost of this text

　　　is subject to sudden hikes sudden inflationary pressures
　　　surfactants in residuals at the copa-copacabana the hottest
　　　press south of the prospect of never quite making it on the
　　　long march through the letter press stapler more pressing
　　　outfit quandry slipper or trainer or brogue

the cost of this text

　　　is mercurial in the extreme subject to periods of languid
　　　spam

the cost of this text

　　　cannot be recouped from the babysitter from sheer loss of
　　　having taken slices extracts from the texture of its loss of
　　　human contact spent in page over screen over the decision
　　　that writing take up the gloss of its priority as the spectacle
　　　of the suspension of the ethical tuned to stations of the
　　　family stop

the cost of this text
> is no demon of the analogy but a vector more digital
> than thou more dreamt in the clam sparking readiness
> to surrender agent blurb the heavy breathing the ain't no
> fountain frank enough but coming to get you

the cost of this text
> is inclusive of the course fee and you will not be required
> to write a report on its many longueurs and white spaces
> singing hey ho the grammarbot

the cost of this text
> whatever it is put a spell on me scuse me while I kiss the sky

the cost of this text
> will be yours for the asking the question made substantive
> turning to the definite phrasal mood scope spun on the
> sixpence of said possessive what's yours is ours is mine again
> not to reason the final pay scheme

the cost of this text
> is to sparsely burn where patterns take the verb to mildly go
> splice no split infinitive where none intended none taken
> none gained and no returns

the cost of this text
> is at its dearest in the stitch sample item in the suture of
> said threaded sky recently kissed just so much for the textile
> dampers outsourced to china

the cost of this text
> is refreshingly modest and to be had for a song a pawn
> broke dust of a rights issue quite reasonable quite in the
> eighth type of ambiguity herein named the party of the first
> and the party of the last quite so quite becoming end quotes

the cost of this text

        has no insurance against livid planes shaving a syntax of
        sweatshop ash in the hacker's gulag now stung by news of
        new old stock bucket brigade chip shift delays held to live
        work deficits sewn into the label as a spine

the cost of this text

        cannot be spelt out in so many words

the cost of this text

        is as powerful as the kind fictions against which revolts
        the active purse so turning a forlorn binding of celluloid
        election for a fixed term without fear of coalition jitters and
        of fear of well fear of the genitive in general

the cost of this text

        will be not free at the point of need unless such need can
        be shown to be so pressing as to bring new urgency to the
        needs of the definite article as in reason not the need

the cost of this text

        is a shadow of its former proofs now thoroughly torn
        between surging cupboards of cliché and unintended leaps
        into after party sales here's to speculative revery enjoyed by
        revolutionary optimists everywhere

the cost of this text

        could blame it on the boogie but will not indulge the reflex

the cost of this text

        will forever evade the question of paying back a percentage
        of its profits to the objects of its unacknowledged
        imperialism

the cost of this text

        can't get you out of its head has more debts than you care

to consider set to inhibit if not prevent easy adoption for
fresh composition on the textbook slop shop thank you for
paying by direct debit

the cost of this text
has not been charged to your account but can be imagined
as a proportion of the total labour expended in the name of
social reproduction divided by the unit cost of its current
production

the cost of this text
will not join hands and form a love train in praise of the
losses

the cost of this text
is a speculative proposition bound to grammar as on a wheel
of reasonable doubts but not half the noun it used to be

the cost of this text
will be mourned as a latter-day privatised elegy for
minimalist tat now on line cooing still to the softer sell
maximalist montage why don't you now set me free why
don't you now

the cost of this text
is not worth waiting up for

the cost of this text
owes a debt of gratitude to sundry fluxus flavours that will
never be paid or tendered that cuts up rough when asked to
declare its position on the future of trident

the cost of this text
is not what you think it might be nor what matters most
in a moist sculpture of definite substantives turning articles
out of goods out of ink

the cost of this text

        cannot be judged by the ragged cover of its scuppered
        photocopy on fibre stall likely as a loss notice in the seriality
        of how oft the perceived film contracts war in the analogue
        just as the get go gets real gets reality

the cost of this text

        does not mean but leans lean on me the leaning
        resemblance to a spontaneous outpouring of secondary
        sentiments puffed up into a price ratio of private incomes
        recollected in the counting houses of tranquility

the cost of this text

        is braced for a critical mauling of mosh pit proportions
        where to be alive is to be quite other than to wish only for
        standing room dead set against constituting itself as a hot
        ticket even for the hottest spot north of Havana

the cost of this text

        does not look like a gift horse that is ready to be messed
        with by the dentists of the imagination

the cost of this text

        cannot be gainsaid even by its closest beneficiaries and
        shows no trace of sharp practices elsewhere priced into the
        plummeting prosody of loyal managers set on reconstituting
        poetry with a capital p what's that spell

the cost of this text

        is a drop in the ocean of full employment

the cost of this text

        does not assert the moral right of its agents of textual
        production to be photographed in disappointing postures
        of eager dissipation a few biscuits short of a fully costed
        deconstruction

the cost of this text
> cannot be offset against the barcode of its carbon
> fingerprints

the cost of this text
> does not mind its own business with increasing signs of
> abating

the cost of the text
> is on the verge of bankruptcy unless and until there is a
> significant reduction in the demands of the private sector
> and a new willingness to wear redistributive vests on sleeves

the cost of this text
> has paid its dues voted for strike action downed tools
> put up and shut up and will play no part in the coming
> academic audit

the cost of this text
> is not tangled up in blue

the cost of this text
> cannot be understood as a fraction of your weekly shop
> but usually works out at something like twice the number
> you first thought of but still less than the minimum wage
> dreamt of by students of the Parnassian gamble

the cost of this text
> is a matter best left to consenting adults studying the
> question of matter as matter with matter and free data
> bundles will fly

the cost of this text
> is cheap as chips the cheaper the faster the micro toxic
> rashers of silicon all creamed to a fuzz

the cost of this text

      is motif summing the narrow now that is the bun dance
shown that is the colour of bank vectors that is the both
with its own logic and relations in morphology bled from its
radius cost of more splits school of political blouses and the
cost of this blusher taped onto due diligence on an itinerary
of triangular livings shed bung in the glitz barn there where
the dream is all piano and Busby Berkeley takes to the
ivories habitual axes gone fishing who is the cost of this
tadpole puritan in same sort antideterminist balloon anyone
for the great spandrel hike their very landscape is the costing
now cross-checking the polka lip on a sufficient pale fumble
the cot rarely occurs in a pure form it is difficult for the
banal to sulk in tapes in hi fatigues no more than passwords
to the cost cutting exercise promised to aerial brooms axes
of passage their exits and their defenses the apartments take
on the cake of the slice now on the level

the cost of this text

      is half party half scam scanner part the mud mauve music
loom way over the asking price and slipper top as from the
mouths of mikes and cameras bleed forth songs of factory
pop cherry sordid in the rope of words

the cost of this text

      is what you make of it and making take for fuel of gutted
irony

the cost of this text

      is subject to deviation from a mean that is so mean as to
be the blouse and just dandy among shoe gazers and pedal
boards let's hear it for dubstep doom taking the bird's eye
tin pan alley dirt scan fuzz test

the cost of this text

      is no match for the tinted orange paypal button wielding

its jump lunge and spandex twitter is as twitter does here
comes the bid for the change trope that's brass in the cash
bar and no matter not that it is matter

the cost of this text

bears no malice against the differentials evident in the
prospects of the haves as against the had and looks forward
to the hands of unelected googlers with the eagerness of a
copy that is fresh and hot

the cost of this text

is not worth the paper it is printed on

the cost of this text

will be way over the odds your inheritance threshold can
embrace but by no means way over the heads of those
wonderful people out there in the dark now ready for the
sweet talk of social justice and border controls

the cost of this text

is as sharp as the cut against the bias of its own love of
textile design

the cost of this text

is not to be had for the price of a burn shaving in a grumble
after more than a week's pocket money blown on digital
persistence amid the screen memories of theory and the
sublime discount qua donate qua crash cuts

the cost of this text

is more than anything a measure of scoured vineyards
porous to telephone broom toes blended into squalid
pickling ores

the cost of this text

is costly does and costly knows a thing or two about

cameras ready or not here come the cuts the cuts so slavishly
bound to be savage or deep or necessary and plural or just
plain daft

the cost of this text
is half a pound of tuppenny rice half a pound of treacle
and half a pound of sterling crises set against bond markets
doing it for the gross as does for rogue statements that's the
way the sub-prime fiscal biscuit goes

the cost of this text
is quite literally priceless summa contra literalists its
underlying economics boosted to barking sub mix scupper
set to audit surplus the picquant tread flamers marches
to mumble infoprole grists set to hack and dung shy of a
bloom

the cost of this text
is reasonable quite the done thing wink tank sic yes surely
do less than the sum of its smart pack less than the plume
of its parting less than the thumb huh baroque let's get
metrical

the cost of this text
is shed friendly and goose to the dérive all dimples
exponentially free at the cusp the scourge of syntax yet
scarcely made it through the steer burns

the cost of this text
is low down the classic notion of strolls quips quiddities
and sunk moon the exit stage mazard gooseneck a slip of
teal into the dripping or stale terrain stuck in grey data
provoking the cost of clog bristle taken to task and sent
zones in this outage so who distills the emotional busker
one of the basic situationist costs of this rapid passenger
ambience curls into

the cost of this text
>   is picking up good vibrations next stop free milk and bus
>   passes

the cost of this text
>   went to bed to mend its head with sellotape and white
>   paper

the weight of this line
>   shadows its origins in a flux of give and take
>   and is taken for what is lighter than 'the' gift
>   that passes for dry biscuits, idols and gloom

the weight of this line
>   stakes its coming derailment in some drive to
>   full stops, *petit morte* now cue sunday drivers
>   before sweet ascension amid sunday painters

the weight of this line
>   goes to ground in the face of soiled life saying
>   what rogue male is the prompt for such gifts
>   what black craft sings kitsch and night pathos

the weight of this line
>   reveals the plangency of spent book keepers
>   set on tongue and groove accumulating slips
>   its royal blue stamp dressing a transparency

the weight of this line
>   cannot bear how waste as modulated prose
>   sits about in a frenzy of margins and grids
>   only to flower up as some option to flame

the weight of this line

       takes up the gift option on its nude inflation
       and sees no call for the flax as money broom
       and lo a retro song of David bent its harping

the weight of this line

       cannot take refuge in the squalls of Moscow
       still storming the winter palace of scumbles
       and spruce which most decorative font is all

the weight of this line

       hears such doggerel as montage in a helmet
       that sings of the vanquished while put spins
       count their blessing as spurned hieroglyphs

the weight of this line

       feels the pressure of press gangs as quantity
       while art house networking in quality goods
       puts nursed ignorance to yet starker reliefs

the weight of this line

       runs up the Brechtian flagpole only there to
       find the flutters of party loyalty too much to
       put in writing like flogging some old Fluxus

the weight of this line

       shirks this work of artsong doing a number
       on its worn tools so that something sweeter
       than flawed fragments become fallen spoils

the weight of this line

       speaks of missives and manifestoes, a retro
       summer held open then snatched back like
       an escapist gift horse loose to grace favour

the weight of this line
        bites the hand that would free luncheon see
        how cloven hearts in mindless misanthropy
        mark the grace spring to void the fruitiness

the weight of this line
        pines for the simplicity of least said soonest
        mended now that bolt on moral cannot give
        but indecent arthood god knows it's private

the weight of this line
        flat lines the 'rock' as a truly dismal header
        done hand to mouth in constant production
        for some renewal of monochrome raiments

the weight of this line
        feels the force of party discipline cut blush
        to severance in relics of selvage, abundant
        bathos in the engineering of earthy canals

the weight of this line
        fondly urges familiar repetition and scars
        sold for cold comfort renewing a monthly
        cycle whose rate of return is replenishing

the weight of this line
        is more asked for than asking, microfont
        does dark metaphor for its calculus then
        insists blackly on reading glasses for all

the weight of this line
        comes to market and silver hound trace
        elements are set to spend a sleepy rust
        that gives up the bank of mum and dad

the weight of this line
        cannot make out the remedy proposed
        in the fine print, well fine catches sums
        and sets to celebrate this guinea worm

the weight of this line
        shines no prosodic searchlight on this
        this how but pauper theory scoops the
        bauble of its darkly contrapuntal faces

the weight of this line
        dances a glut singing hey liggers how
        does your garden praxis grow contra
        mammon slash Saatchi close brackets

the weight of this line
        will not write to its measure nor bow
        to the gilt and bond market, but puts
        its shoulder to a rights issue pending

the weight of this line
        can be measured in spoons, a spoon
        for every kissed glue or postcard op
        how the message sticks the medium

the weight of this line
        blunders about in junk shops where
        news still filters in from its situation
        in escapism sugared by this prompt

the weight of this line
        calls upon relatives of the giving
        sort to resemble the sense even
        to tax this double dip recession

the weight of this line
        resembles the increasing use of
        increasingly note its press pack
        now in other news marked late

the weight of this line
        puts paid to laws of diminishing
        returns as yet unknown in a rate
        of profit that falls and then sighs

the weight of this line
        sings a living wage in how even
        its most feeble accommodations
        are a part and parcel made good

the weight of this line
        calls forth clam shell castanets
        just as this mouth bites in time
        to amuse their weight watchers

the weight of this line
        begs to differ from the seams
        the stapled blundering digits
        the never feels movable type

the weight of this line
        fills a heavy demand brace
        as its weeping willow goes
        to ground to found capital

the weight of this line
        tires of its heavy conceits
        as what fruits are bloody
        fresh mints for deadlines

the weight of this line
        takes note of said given
        seizure as glass ceilings
        take but gutter to heart

the weight of this line
        shrugs off the quipless
        quango of an imagined
        given still up for taking

BURNT LACONICS BLOOM

CORSAGE
for Dell

(A) CHINESE LANTERNS

find our way in restricted
parade of deadline averted
till the natural drops off
but imagine constraints as
friends, some, even, offer
to rest gainful employment
in their ironed shirts for
factory walls for payslips
for erasures will clock on
now take which dream barge
to establish the contrails
burnt into storage folders
the avatars dragging along
citations, implicating you
are put upon sure but come
on, shiftly, there is less
to be in getting something
as the camera dollies back
you will still lucky lucid
now hold to the microphone
book the tool jumper which
gets our mood a make shift
not artsong, not for you a
lieder cue credits, prizes
but shoots done some bloom

how for you read ours that
is ever growing the hedges
thrown to the wind to fire
indifference in colleagues

(B) LILLIES OF L'INFORME

then again, embrace your
deadline sewing as reams
of tire what mean become
the part song than which
prepositions in becoming
well become mark wrinkle
and more deep than suave
how will be our pleasure
to overthrow gene slaves
and murk in flamboyances
the curing agent is long
in the making, the tooth
minus love of the resumé
you are invited to party
and turn to the flatness
anticipated in gerundive
a future passive purring
you call to calling home
schools and in the ruins
of the lineage of no law
that goes by the name of
daddy where did we leave
off in singularity spent
before braced commitment
so pressing to fall into
the better to best smile
down a culprit meter set
to count for lost pulses

(C) PETIT CHOU-FLEUR

a genealogy of correctives
becomes torpid for blanket
bans on proscenium feeling
show the tendency of tulip
to mutate their allegories
of capital mania to endure
before the bulb sings: oil
this is my painted stretch
my canvas, my urge to turn
all white the charred vein
as taps into this striated
tie pleased to stay in the
designated species in case
some blessedness wished on
each remarkable blemishing
becomes a sweet aberration
not our plunging sarabande
my little cauliflower, our
prospect standing ovations
to applaud looser horizons
the plaster chiselled away
a semblance of archaeology
back to the galleries that
sleeplessness forsook stop
pass what muster slums sew
to become not some alembic
then but our adjectives we
were looking for to defuse

(D) PURPLED EUCALYPTUS

doesn't go to colour down
the many constraints that
the tester is what passes
for quality come trickles
that malady of mannequins
in sequins while to crisp
linen lingering syllogism
is scrupulous rather than
shift to the pleat strife
stripe pleat regular dart
in pearled pins ascending
it doesn't so much a more
than a spectacular outfit
that still makes of party
one worth this waiting up
for the very scope of the
hedginess otherwise a hem
sustaining marginal songs
that cannot live down the
gulf between monopoly and
hope but just to reassert
the question of l'informe
gone digital in artefacts
there's love in our stuff
the mad things hoarded up
for aliasing to boot then
so so softening synthesis
before jump cut to jumble
firing on all overlockers
you can't be sure of less
to be still more becoming

COO COW COWPERS

sadly to salt winds
inflamed fell skies
and remained low
to cliff get heights
that's terrible look
down from though
down would dash
to pieces has been
best for the shrunk
bound to precipice
the harsh house in
bears a name sock
poppy lands brief
days well all days
of delight dune to
sing song blighters
have you got light
boy heard to haar
to buggy rummage
then not me neither

THE ANECDOTAL TURN

slam dunk critical reads
commodity methodism
into tyrannical medium
flaming bland and peril
which stale breath gales
how a theory flags a bit
falling into a descriptive

but even a were to wish
what would so were that
wished to were but even
were the being it would
not be worn from where
nor the who would be a
body without organs nor
that fish heads trimming
sometimes it is necessary
to cut oneself off at root

CAESURAE AND BALLROOM BELLINIS

'*FORGET that you live in houses, that you may live in yourself –*'
Mina Loy (Aphorisms on Futurism)

virelay: drayton gloss: colons
ambergris: so to use: perfumes
battening: said to boo: thrive
bellwether: minims: lead sheep
chapelet: billions: wreath for
clip: the hand lounge: to kiss

crankling: fees eh: lets twist
dowset: knitted pretty: doucet
estridge: took flight: ostrich
frouncing: thats lol: frizzing
hind: the living bung: peasant
impresa: still tridents: motto

kelled: the douche nod: webbed
leven: in demo mode: lightning
mell: to bruise: mingle meddle

orpharion: gutless: lutes then
penny-feather: tootling: miser
roundelay: goose jig: refrains

simple: ballroom bellini: herb
stover: with chips: snowy grub
taw: dodecaphonic swab: to tow
ure: short-lined to spend: use
whig: the glosses: butter milk
zany: in mounting panic: mimes

*

toggles: fanshawe notes: semis
cancelled stanza: starrs: cute
or gaudy: vide puppies: waters
betting or firing: doe: vetted
reliques: be broyl'd again: or
one upshot: sayle: tinged with

verdicts: fanning windes: pure
white: can still this: mangled
semantic: blankers: degen'rous
place holder: lofty: strangely
itself a toggling: mickle: air
with this: this merely: sticks

by nature: merely petal: souls
slight variant: printed: error
in purse: who wound: as inward
dimme: dimm'd: latin'd obscura
shogge: shoogled: side to side
dravell'd: wet of saliva: made

to engrayle: rough: or prickly
indented edge: margin: a sheet
roaping: dumbing up: thickened
would: as in wou'd: then wooed
lother: taken to: print rather
source: not identified: a plat

*

beyond seas: lovelacing: turns
blue-god: phone hacks: Neptune
to make better: groom: sensing
clue: googlers: ball of thread
the common suage: hip: assuage
sarabandes: then: triple timer

to nard: sans microsoft: aroma
gilt-plaits: red top: patchier
cozening: sweet tabbed: cheats
clouded: literally: in the sky
the minikin: studious: trebles
in buskins: satellite tv: boot

box or show: sludger: sexed up
boorein: see page 3: a peasant
in gyves: now kettled: fetters
incarnadine: as dogs: to flesh
motions: that to folk: puppets
green-god: fire truck: Neptune

his queen: all egg: Amphitrite
crisping: mid chariot: curling
neat: pass the duchies: cattle
hallowed: be thy demo: hollows
antic: the looter blue: absurd
gust: the disputed bill: taste

TALK STRING
for John Cage

'*Hedges are informal, less specific markers of probability or uncertainty.*'
                                                            Douglas Biber

in praise of indeterminacy
in prose of co-determinacy
soldier flarf fluff signed
to recoup the originals in
blends a dash friend stash
margin so saying scribbles
pregnant pauses out of the
box marks squadron private
THAT deletion is in clause
pied piping here in swarms
the that salient loading a
head in clefted tagging as
he had been warning before
how reception as per moles
in quandary of poison mush
rooms such as centurion or
frigates or downtoners who
gives some shift into mood
less certain even livelier
against a general emphatic
still that is touch and go

WAGED MINIMALISM

ah, the smell of syntax in the morning
as for rust belts so saying apocalypse
well shoulder to shoulder with scandal
and finds wingers smarting in shifters
like this: not for nothing does a dawn
go off on one toasted all night thread
buttoning up for a tailor set in satin
and not for nothing this: the artifice
of the bird library takings of caw caw
how shirt dart poisons draw raw cupids
well the trial of drone dancing fiasco
would smell as burnt by any other noun
such is the prism of now felt to flame
then left for a dead ringer in shrouds
one more pyjama party giving contrails
of mirage or mig or apache or hercules
for preference strike is the sing song
fit to raise the noise floor spartacus
before taking the drill phrase to task

OF BY WITH OR FROM *WRITING*
for Tom Raworth

this unimagined look comes to in scarf
ah now there they have us by the lichens
please be patient till the system sinks
till a resumé eats flickers doing in cuts
going frame to frame the minute spider
by not some actor egg mooning sequin
plumes are my ghoul my rubber or just

my the whim does takes past art parks
do the seven sisters in greased postcard
dirty analogies tutting précis, merely
interesting as a poem says insecticide
shortened to a lining oh be quick slips
slipping into a comfortable something
we are the contemporaries the crazed
glue gang so wanting nonadministered
justice so no-one left to read subtitles
now even Hollywood does without for
the Marseillaise with fear well shiver
me pinko stumbling thane a failed quip
don't answer the bookish beige singlet
being no foreground for Marcel Proust
to meet Alain Delon in blued badinage
while admitting only fears now signing
away go parapluies o uptown primaries
do a body sites from squatted syntax as
any old mad lib gets a procedural rehab

READING ACROSS

reading across the satirical
something else that isn't as
read but highly theorised as
questioning which is good in
one way image taking biscuit
sense the limited persuasive
did start well just petering
out over said brink glossing
in impressive focus the have
the aggregate the profile as
violence is this fascination

romancing the real kind that
does as you did expect steer
clear of cultural history in
examined celebrations of the
land in a tendency to witter
gasps of coffee before gloom
screech of calm spread range
evidently borderline is flip
the sophists were not really
so sophisticated as anaphora
murks needed in context link
soon upon felt blindness our
down to the sump is the mark

MICROPHONICS
for Pussy Riot

main features bias switch gain
tone control drive and master
of the fowl and brute timidity
power break speak attenuator
but when said box come open
out jumps junior head badge
surprise surprise same factory
same printed circuit board the
pile of faults adding this nice
extra amid the transformation
now extremely articulate and
detailed with a fair amount of
clean headroom punchy sings
quick to lively response curve
you get classic crunch marvels
such warm harmonics then not

not the stuff the transistor ever
heard but full and rich natural
break up blowing off creamy
distortion in negative feedback
while the sustain just flows on

COMMITTING APPOINTMENTS

structuralist heart of my research
now now broke into lead time swans
they ref you up your prof and pops
dissolving characters perhaps more
trauma work can script an analysis
in an end point situated firmly in
the more become so big in Mandarin
like throws too much with one word
one thought is attachment slippage
in fascinator become distanciation
this one failed to attend to broke
hearts in lieu of well show me art
footled with well frankly anything
that can string a sentence blushes
to kiss the one size fits all boot
up the Brechtian for institutional
beyond each audit thing so getting
the numbers up all down said dirty
sure it is indeed dangerous to get
saddled on that basis though which
feet stamping on bland resemblance
to idea will not curdle with specs
and further particulars that dance
or spin that burnt tenured wishing

ERRATICS

ambients score to dark shut
trivia as which calls silence
at no point frees up evening
but in background city map
falls to shutter speed darns
so to this structuring as shut
before scoring out a hipster
done sunnier the event face
left by the traction glassing
into yellow tungsten mirrors
and not before time you not
don't preferring ampersand
as but might be callousness
is not the shark to take it for
old friend returning to murk
in it fold the interest bit that
anything called bits as wind
to make up conjunctions as
said wart bloom enthusiasm
for darts the nonconformism
held to heart where none go
dancing the shaft squall piss
how up is the mood bleach

PEARL SANS EAR RINGS

mother of grant am I
the middle felt same
tawny then interests
spread to gee troops

gallery context am I
only to say revealed
non hedging splurges
romancing quick loan
selfless rich artist
wanted vampires need
only apply then sing
spruce sheets are we

LICHENS FOR MARXISTS

NEWS FROM LICHEN TIMES

many rivers to cross
many lichens to sing
many refugees to see
and shelter in night
when the nightfisher
swims against a tide
that is dark capital
    is the song the same
    when in western wind
    the drones are funds
    in a month of ballad busting
    lunar toting dusty columns
        here at the poetics of
        limit comrades this is
        some defeaning blur in
        saying but why grammar
        does no stone nor even
        the rose as in present
        making up the clearing
storm the material then immateriality
falls into lineage with the relations
striking socialism's symbiotic drifts
now play standards dreaming and vinyl
        over this raised playground
        all is lichen star symbiotic
        tars and proletkult morphemes
        hollering ahoy there oxygen

scalded be but screeds coming
on strong when the bombs fall
there will low down criminals
bites for what can be but ire
gone senseless in people talk
      which came first
      Marx and Spenser
      or truth to song
      the blister logs
      talking of barks
      come plantations
      the whole croppy
      punk punctuating
      a lichen gooding
  when the weave
  words to fosse
  how the lichen
  born with cups
  gives etruscan
  melody bearing
we in symbiotic alliance of lichen
hold the evident truth to the self
namely that all lives are not made
the same and the carbon liberation
front will be the death of all but
the persistent solidarity of algae
now and in the calendar of lichens
    every eve is new
    every time is wild
    every birthday is a return to first principles
        before the eating of carbon cakes or
        musical statues and acid rain takes the
        biscuit to show us the way to darkest
        reserves as lark relics made into airs
            honey sound does

sun money bounds
over car dusters
and sunk capital

LICHEN CARD

but least two organisms
fungus or mycobiont and
a partner or photobiont
from either sweet green
sewn different kingdoms
how names we call mossy
but not in any way like
not in any way a strong
though sung association
gives the picture after
the photomorphs so fade
the bulk is visible out
with the pollution done
out with the sold pores

SONG OF THE UNKNOWN GRAPHEME

context is all quoth the linguist
down to a native speaker who wept
punctuation is but said lichen of
your discontents made ruly matter
can there be but words enough for
the imperial litter bullet points
and this stark fungi of asterisms

yes punctuation is such lichen of
your dissertated content drifting
into sentence laws of the thallus
imposing clouds of graphematicity
in inscription of an anthropology
as befits no colon worth its semi
lozenge now no obelus nor pilcrow
yes capitals do brand our science
and to put too fine a point on it
there is no linguistics worth its
cognate that doesn't fall in with
punctuation and in so falling who
hears the I sing that accompanies
all our silent misrepresentations
and passes such as silence dashed

SANG OF THE UNKENT LICHEN

the crack is wall spored a lichen
fax to a fungal partner who shone
bacteria as but the rift crust is
mossy free living not algal bloom
how little or no is to type still
crustose foliose and fruticose oh
beard moss unfurl a broken cortex
and deictic vegetative propagules
yes lichen is such punctuation of
even a pre-cambrian morph to gold
into a colonising as conjunctions
in prescriptions of an industrial
revolution calling for apostrophe
yes heavy metals do kill our kind
polluting the lost veneer on aged

buildings as to punctuate the air
there is no lichen scale but maps
in pulls of sulphur dioxide a new
poverty and so many cryptic moths
there past hydrogen flouride sing
who could survive the nuclear war
down wind of the unsung prolepsis

EPIPHYTES & NEOPHYTES

a fungus and a photosynthetic
symbiont in stable vegetative
structure being body specific
the cell walls discovering in
mutual agriculture an extreme
for deserts to a tune of many

they find crusty leafy frondy
squamulose even leprose quite
demeaning in a typical growth
from the human naming project
despite a grave marker energy
giving symbiosis to semantics

which ultimate pioneer plants
reveal food to reindeer moose
and deer and flying squirrels
from the snub-nose monkeys of
China to rock tripe explorers
and for starvation provisions

turning famine worlds dust to
manna from heaven as a desert
lichen served by the wind for
still dyes perfumes medicines
poisons and litmus a doctrine
of signatures proving colours

now still radioactive fallout
falling on fields even as the
move of marine to terrestrial
life in the Proterozoic Eon's
not so boring billion but for
earth's clueless late species

THE ADJECTIVAL LICHEN

a braille to natural history
what with even missile nouns
struck by the exemplar lance

brute colours sewn to sharps
ramifying in the spiller toe
all set to lie tufted sponge

once made do got along scaly
even in frankly opake matter
in the din that so squanders

that is the lit wallow turfy
some said notched this mealy
adjective into the making do

down to firing or granulated
in the brushed call of seems
come stall but creeping fire

who would true fertile force
find each zigzag locker song
quite friable in the musters

in symbiosis spilling spores
over the less sinuated parks
and the tremble of the braid

NO TAXONOMY WITHOUT REPRESENTATION

languishing in a dense texture of blooms
the lichens in old grammar speak volumes
quite literally some arcana and pantheon
all duals and plurals and distant solids

parcels even in the cloud sign who knows
what falls how sad as by the passing sky
it is some nature to conjure with amidst
the fry up formally unfurled as progress

every kidded kidder combing his maturity
in an assigned wood song so quaintly put
my my how the growth spurt is the killer
pull the other carbon and taste in peats

the colour of symbiosis shown irony bans
will take what sun tide face to rosettes
now that nature is dead in still remains
and so on to the dawn of gathered plumes

LICHEN PROSPECTUS

specimen leaves sung down for pages
in the desert of the analogy longed
for as only a condition of elephant
paper similes with the microcosm of
the hot press amidst the temples of
the spirit going down down and mute

how botanical plates scan the vying
even as nature itself copper plates
or adds a florist and public bodies
subscribers as yet deficient tuning
toward a delicacy of the engravings
the deception no throne to complete

such heights became the bold lichen
from Plato to Tesco the whole money
rolling into genera named scripture
of the root radical in which office
in print the highest style executes
and embellishments slew into papers

the money lyrics illustrating fatal
attraction as wild promissory notes
go in minor mood to mock prospectus
it is at best whispers in symbiosis
growth rates in a month of moondays
whose litmus does landskip and dyes

FAST TALK

when fast talking lichens rule the roost
and lack any semblance of ready wit fire
shy nothing gives it large on cold stone
not to endure but to define public forms

and not realised gilts not even the cash
but verbal minimalism the maybes uh-huhs
all well and good the laconical deprives
as the sally sets up quips or air mottos

zones marked salty put down in acid rain
who knows types ungrammatical but strong
sound kisses are the democratic children
what we shall here term a voice plus one

VALUE COMB

with some hesitation this
value of the lichen combs
and why x does matters so
that we've had our fun is
now specific to the viols
billowing into endolithic
vocal hyphae thread-bared
to be into sunny openings
there's the eyes in sound
made by something as soul

xanthoria to you or yours
spectacular latinity swab
swatch so long dying well
the scars a ripped breach
mats in to thinned futons
will you be ours in rifts
my drift as topper leaves
our crust evening into an
unlearning blank opposite
the lunar hulk or carcass

a some such so slow wound
in snow toes strung among
proofs to the presence of
the hung gruel done flame
in the morphology of calm
murk could be our jumpers
for in lithographic henge
the passages from realism
to ism subtend a scarcity
a bent car in leafy grits

mm with an inch of a life
of air rolls over to tuck
in now which lichens call
syntax ungrounded a choke
chain in no a need spokes
run to brittles just keep
sunny side up with quicks
to soft tain of this rock
this ribbon to soft crust
will to wilt done sulphur

ALLOA LICHENS
for John Goodby

matter keeps blossoming so
as grimes or hasty lunatic
dreams Eve's shaggy creeps
lining patter of pith tilt
down a fluid blade of rags
it's become ecclesiastical
all influenced by Mallarmé
seraphim tears faint viols
of sadness as satin waking
is to be the morning nymph

stars in your trousers and
bogus tribe of sad opacity
aye right but my own stuff
reads bitter satire on ego
doing primitive echolation
the analog stymie kangaroo
down books for gout toxins
for shed red read candy to
to tone up a terse preface
for horrible introductions

backflip anarchist kissing
is some cosmic punctuation
reduced to proxies glazing
clarty data carving sweat
freezer scanning sentiment
insert new line here sweet
formica rim sill call what
is the firmament never now
a get out of the page cage
through text to word worms

the slurs to pastel drench
in engagements with a word
there's no shame making an
honest work of parts larks
processing the opened riot
its bank junk mail shelved
even a people on the shelf
own it sharpen your tippex
a measure will deal fairly
will make new wilted bills

documentary's the key word
here for faked locality to
cite the celtdom tains and
symboliste forays centaurs
current in electrification
passing through collective
ballets hence converted to
socialism in ecliptic turf
tail physical to fit small
high towers in subtle tint

night lies to embed a mute
parterre or metal peacocks
who else thinks the sun is
alive and shining marauder
melts under bronze thistle
colour things speaks gorse
as when the sound puts its
room just where people are
roaming their meanings and
that's not my nose too off

as rhubarb breaks out glad
rags, this one is untitled
all hail impossible genres

stub of syntax deep middle
the turtle long pink tooth
to look emboldening silver
white pigeons to be abject
so static falls fail words
the tough aromas of Diageo
blending away to ash cloud

slow Longannet Grangemouth
sluice down garderobe flow
courage up we're so sludge
and beautiful we're an oil
painting, a Castalian band
just be the miracle as you
are translation with paper
the effs have the how goes
for here this is not radio
and loud all ways too loud

trojan horses for the cube
waltzing surreal not sense
this to call scream casual
the fault buckle and break
folk and fauna, flock high
you can google it everyone
does in shut eyed defiance
against dead law to tyrant
radio dial snatchers where
no name is a great fiction

not native but inhabitants
sing fear of contradiction
even for a darkest morning
the birds do sing breaking
into song vandals blending
Nietzschean impeachment oh

what gives Jock lit., what
gives, will it be soil the
numpty stock ressentiments
ah fuck it and begin again

no more of Brechtian stuff
ye say do awa or roses and
spelling a larger Damascus
out of Rosa Luxemburg with
an anecdotal basking shark
the cliff top killer lines
are not at all imaginative
on the fantastic green and
embroidered lichens of the
Castalian band in slippers

red army & green Parnassus
a.k.a. the Ochils tendency
let slip to chorus morning
as at dancing waters meets
still clip and riff chasms
fluxus burns of care water
rising for the baldness of
all but such fit humanists
how the great hypermarkets
of Alloa tune the swallows

SILICON GLITCH

quick and dirty solutions fox in rust
or find lit nights for global blights
all plastic pyres over decaying plant
over every lichen lettered windowsill

each ecological niche
grown into its island
of carbon cliché sung
by the inch worm tort
such retrograde farming, human growth
over the factory of scripted willings
down take that stabs at time off from
dreamt emissions with the city filter
bright bleed and even
excessive collections
become severed treats
to such went existing
meanwhile sheep in Libya graze on low
aspicilia esculenta and even in Japan
umbilicaria settles down in salad and
in deep fried fat not to mention cars
as to still democracy
can't live up scenery
for class war etching
into the grassy ditch
and the heavy fireworks that flounder
amid new calls for lichen sanctuaries
falling on ears set to leafless right
stacked before our cup runneth nought
how come cash is kept
coming up checker tie
for a megaphone drawl
made out to franchise
some taste fridge in kettle's kitchen
done cut brass to scallops so clogged
and in flames for the planet's collar
all silk sung stains gone to liveries
even strange will say
the musk bark liquids
cannot turn substrate
over a global vitrine

over lost vellum, over gelatin hooves
sleep lost in a mercurial now falling
short into mud slung footnotes & lows
then take that turn for the burst sun

LICHENS FOR LEVELLERS

among bitter cups as were man
a grand brush dipt in whiting
the utter crackling of credit
plagues the formalist and how
   grosse error in the press
   can be nothing to paction
   over column inches a then
   the magnifie so imbracing
   stead cloud of Iuno State
to hair cloth and mystery and
already much sope, much nitre
would sparkle phang and pawes
poore, clad with patcht clout
sheets, very narrow ones also
so cast to have all in common
   spoils, effusion of bloud
   moliminous, body contrary
   scaffold the long groaned
   general to Junto idolatry
put upon strange thing as you
made freely, one with another
land rather be broke not kept
no interest as breathing will
with the much cozened lapwing
   for ought yet a body else
   reap thereby a doubt army

by hearsay thistles never
bore figs of freedome the
beds of down estate serve
war like bruit beast have
to heart what a present slave
under dominion states trouble
notwithstanding the vast pang
after this blossom of liberty
bitter fruit in vile bond
sight unseen, folk lichen
upright mountain cladonia
spartan or spartacist art
they of the many theys called
you a terrorist, a red thread
gone through as stole of life
spent in some cell, some yard
read into a deadening history
that absolves none from waste
but stood tall and smiling to
put the brave face struggling

PREPOSITION STRANDING

up with this put will not put
orders standing by or dowsing
lichen put to stroll wordsing
not downs gone to the crevice
but nevertheless shoulders in
limestone ark, a spelt strain

grip & tackle to long sweeper
reaching to a deft croft lode
told as the substance quality

in the leaf of the noun stems
obedience to a marginal gloss
let's say unexpressed opening

but to shape that gives slash
very much their own dimension
the watershed for stone logic
even to some brink of spheres
fairly elementary grammar and
became what is had to be said

love to hear about super type
metal pepsi well newly bolder
and not even really modistics
but under is name seme of the
speculative this is not it at
all at all this is the strand

flowering to swung manuscript
soon to die out in a Prisican
wave moon falters how gravity
is your friend not a sun turn
drift to lie grounds rounding
the so slung shadow principle

new texts are themselves over
whelmed to still a curriculum
is theory style split of good
to which a whom that referred
to in sum the tools can light
the front loaded trope tiller

indebted to the noun style as
no not broad is a-floundering
as per figures tropes oh know

the rest cut light or dogstar
whether day ever is spread or
stranded on give over to mode

down with what is this soiled
in a turn about the allusions
they know the hell not to wet
and forget the spelling check
that tickers and flickers and
goes slow to sew a form spore

even hundred words per minute
is not too few you do to sums
no never say never leads into
errors trap one civil matters
go to socianism go to smudges
as a litter letters socialism

so fallible is a failing grip
your stemma in ours a scourge
caution to the wind as homing
the harming taken to be tasks
extinct yes that's the rub as
in bookends fire family lines

verses became bullets in hand
to hands protestantism spirit
rock breaking in font bashing
into the purely shatter midge
to midge tracking the carbons
but crawling about the erring

that scratch bramble into bit
per bit dipping this variorum
into rubble ruff gods a goner

who bloods the name to pumice
or greenly spun into fair air
r.i.p. parallelism concurring

LETTERS FROM EDINBURGH

'they talk very grammatically'
Edward Topham

some deluge loafing letter
rose mouthing that capital

to rank or drawn facsimile
through dark stays exposed

to sale and the herb women
shunning the heavy hand of

drysalters how said lichen
did each storey of land as

a house is in the sensible
dressed macaroni home spun

as all stone of brown cast
runs down the great swifts

in painted pattern figures
of commodities sold within

so fond of glaring colours
but a plaintive simplicity

in the general of the song
and many sable processions

foxed trappings and blazes
how empty founds in formal

panegyric shall beg stupid
to leave the letter in yrs

CROTTLE SONG

lichens turn brilliant textile dyes
and the brilliance is no colloquial
fix or rust bled in a colour purple
but ancient garment without mollusc
deaths and in the orchil tendencies
as in a sad robe excavated in China

and just as there's no true romance
in murex the cheap labour set dying
young so on in bronze and iron ages
to the lawns of cudbear and crottle
the crystal that fouls the gears oh
and fecal matter amid graith tweeds

in the end it is some famous beauty
dealt in a depletion a scar harvest
a lie in economic growth that kills
growth lent sheen by double dipping
the biblical in blood flags and not
lichens freed at the mouths of need

LICHEN / UNLICHEN

brittle as throttled spawn
consoling terminal trojans

the spill to digital locks
burns to the cult figurine

tick over amplified blades
scrolls into sinking heart

a certain strain of affect
theory replicating fallacy

into schema cues to genera
the visceral tax on naming

viz heather rags as stolen
in the geistliche bruising

upstairs does sponge broom
listing and indeed a frown

a naval lichen turning out
native insight the food of

hibernating arm pragmatism
ersatz activism in digital

fields so the care quality
now giving tone on natural

betraying the anxious leaf
its present affective body

permeable by lung trifling
yes trifled is as does the

quota of mercy given felts
each to brutal informality

GOLDEN TWENTIES

in solar microscopes upon the
screen of white paper bloomed
unsatisfactory representation
you cannot experience the sun
filaments now reduced to damp
done squat in mild amplitudes

moments of worsted land known
by the ennui of the precision
obtaining the data for damper
teeth of complete dark spread
to a friction radiation diode
and poor unconvincing results

aiming at destabilization the
sponsor is the bouncing spoil
so much in probability arrays
so disturbing we run to sleep
sheep over spleen over screen
spred thinner than doing does

the drift failure trial plays
dog-whistle racism then bling
buffs up the brevity to slurs

over the bridge to mild pains
where innovation is the noise
lie who will not stay in true

while the commentariat drives
into the sunset as a deadline
the ether slows up every rain
into the more palpable gating
agog over results of eclipses
baying that no-one need worry

REWILDING YIELDS

part animal, part beast the lit
ecology of lichenometry heralds
poésie pure's extinction lining
gloss quantum musing with frond
in pretences imposing paradigms
on every speculative hedge fund
slow bled into relative reveals

not just a crisis in old physic
though that too, but relativity
of grammars bending word-worlds
and the wit is furious quick so
much to be desired, well facile
when the sustain nose calls for
footnotes now butter over bread

this way lies scurvy, not photo
synthesis or in general pull of
the moon to historical bounties
a statistical minimum prospects

in truth, personality in flames
to justify to the funding hound
the panoply of aesthetic supper

then aspect in play or chiasmus
our ontological bouncer in song
this quantum hump horizon, call
it what you will but out of the
dust cloud comes every definite
article spent on wrecks the new
not so playful nor merely messy

rigour as the parameter of same
again and again till the ambits
set hard in concrete universals
praxis just for its own sake as
in experiments that heat a word
but no demon of this analogy to
resemble a species in lab-coats

the loungers cut the coat-tails
to spite their theories without
remainders a one such remainder
being love of form, a dupe lord
of positivism also known as the
fallacy, constitutive formalism
does smell as high, just not so

trial and error goes to a tough
judgment court among clattering
bills when the word paint flies
even unto a sorry pillowbook no
it won't do, it is not just the
form guide to lived experiences
then again for gravity as prose

by concepts of procession moons
the espousing, seek some grouse
if not the thinking we at first
then once then never once again
be our republic well the merger
calls fug, fog and fakery words
subject to rendition or torture

PROOF IN THE LITMUS

some things cannot be stated too clearly
for to want of urgency can kill the very
conditions of the possible there alerted
such as the crushing of the anthropocene
turned hypha done to the double genitive
as who pummels the always already not so
human into submission and then not thing
things so much as the alms of the farmer
transpositions in cultivations of scarce
done moss cotton and meat for the living
which compasses proud things round about
and finds the weather changing too quick
too unaccommodated in the ungodly brutal
such as cannot see the souls for lichens
and cannot be but some spirit given bone
and invisible but for prying microscopes
a cut glass sheen turning dead lights on

as the acclaim hurts an evidence
making furrows that might become
monitors of pollution staring at
the lit key turning the vitrines
and not even fastness in rancour
can assemble culls into big data
        but light hammers for any old nail
        exploding into archives of answers
        greedy for brighter event horizons
                as focus gives
                it taketh away
                back and forth
                in sweet firth
                lay vivid till
                the song sings
        its serving engine angles festoons
        on to Cambridge rocking microtomes
        how after the stain, balsam mounts
how radial enclosure fields this current crop
how real feeling bled into the making of this
        this demonstrating incision, lines
        in the fold of all violence or ill
        rules for parasitic questions that
        call into classing the thank blood
                down sulphur pulls for
                siestas by vivid moons
                these still explosions
                were never quite still
        nor brisk high tones of pragmatism
        merely open to the worker with the
        requisite skills to mark slaughter
        in some percentage of dead empties
        done to ladder each civil dialogue

bad mouthing as lichens
to blaspheme the earths
speechless for capitals
become dark water stars

     in dappled strings
     soldered to linger
     by cloud varieties
     laddering grammars

lichens as concrete poems to built
brutalism with the islands of said
markets recognising no water marks
as colonies and territory choppers
macro more's the pity of dull bias

     where the smile becomes
     fluid tropes for twists
     in on swallows clusters
     for bright murmurations

how the bland, featureless spore is but
drab from crumbles, spindles, a pattern

     lichen arias, sing to
     scraping in the dark
     capital on the make

like the pathetic fallacy making a home from
home in the artefact of entire affect stocks
for butter candy in signposts of the scissor

     lichen arias, hoop to
     lungs in the purple
     steeps in the wrath

for a keepsake made do standing in with
universal suffrage of the lichen canals
that are bound to some difference grant

     draft drift sing deftly
     till the song is an end
     in ourselves, yes, even
     to the rust of recorded
     pride, limestone or sun

VOTE LICHEN

the lichen poem amalgamating natures
has left no stone unturned or unsung
even unto the pits of grime's graves
each picturesque set has been harmed
in the making of our romancing troop
and stigmata of printed mutter in on
materiality as lichens gloss revenge

so saying I am Caesar of darker wood
in a land now forever lichen, oh not
half you chisel headed facepalm scar
thus spake Debbie in algorithmic mud
the lordly so isolate satyrs conjoin
a finite carry on in penny dreadfuls
for they are these darker song birds

the still of the worm nothing lichen
spring curl and mettle swarf o emoji
ideologeme the proud stone lip syncs
with a few jars and ozymandian brews
in every spore how neither thermidor
nor reforestation can save us from a
winsome horror of hapless allegories

to forever industrial oh happy burns
spelt from spelling walls the lichen
falls for none but the sulphur songs
and many happy revellings shouldered
the revival letterboxes doing oxygen
to fenestrate in light so many bothy
ballads, so many happy rusted trails

sing a song of four and twenty black
words shining then into pale logging
unnatural law for an ode against the
odds, solidarity sounds so recursive
and so sung the symbiotic song roots
justice in a monospaced font there's
no reconciling a pixel dirt embraced

filaments or spores among siren suns
every black mountain grown epiphytic
sigh and a gaze over the fault lines
from Alloa to Faslane now no nuclear
would sail but did still print water
this rock this sky to folk artichoke
the many to lark in some sunny niche

LICHEN BEACONS
for Tom Hall

come closer till seen by its own light
this lichen sees you with your digital
environment turned to face the sunless
capes of our digital code you need not
master but can begin to hear as in now
soundings from a long lived revolution

quite turning and turned again towards
the quantum stroke and dizzy scintilla
whose fossil flint and neolithic skins
take bone from rock battered seashells
crooning with the slime mould in algae
sheening and then revolving into darks

is this the niche on which hoping sits
to gather sun for the autumn crispness
when obliquity is surviving by waiting
which easy street might smell as sweet
by any other name how candy rock tiles
are tooth in bridle to make good decay

but perhaps there can be hearing looks
without a name cover over logic boards
without the whole brand human taxonomy
trading to render unto the sample lord
xanthoria about does it if you need to
name the excrescence of the photosynth

ditto steps back without fear of chalk
or favour save the fire escape parking
a way out from some retail opportunity
where the car stains even blunt frames
calling for sustainable uppers scandal
yes but each spring is so entertaining

to do the wow and ask for less to suns
the yet friends of our digital futures
no kidding it might boil down to likes
and the orange rosette is squashed the
better for love of the tones that dare
some slur of gold upon car park bricks

after a fashion at any rate of imagine
that some darkness staining by ancient
glass how long does it take each glass
to dry out and fall brittle into ruins
in lead pipes or a shattering emoticon
or two as if reviewing the pagan rites

it takes longer for a lichen to set up
residence or anything resembling roots
well the terms simply don't do analogy
and nothing sticks to the distant grip
but the take up substrate is no owning
matter that flags down reference grids

the bond winters into its ring binders
doing mutuals over the parasitic lunch
becoming gloss over stone or riff raff
you know the sort that sees only foods
in the landskip or skulking does poach
from the question of who owns this air

is it Marxism for lichens you are sold
on and upselling into an art star bank
to be installed on every curated index
every forgotten rolodex where the font
of ink has become a drop down security
a rosette for a depreciation of values

the water runs off where it will where
the call of the blue draws its smiling
over the vanity of human summers which
cookie you are obliged to tick box now
so that all your details can be stored
rendered unto food hygiene and capital

take a seat or a pew or the park bench
if you will and cannot stand for birds
the catch in the wind giving some lark
doing the like for immediate broadcast
if you won't and trash the misty dawns
for seen trolls of some hype or bother

many lichens make light work so saying
the grammar can wait for the catch all
reason whistling the same old same old
one sky over flutters and bearded twig
calling for some solidarity to embrace
a quite bitter turn over among dongles

shoulder to shoulder goes the wet ruin
beside the metal on a jet black medium
will it be some party or even postures
on a rocky blog where the spore stands
and falls uncounted by the best before
the burning ask engraved in the taking

THE LOST MOONS OF
ENDYMION THE THIRD

it begins painting night larks
a rustic dross in repeat sleep
towelling vegetarian pantheism
to be shaded nebula and slicks
on drums how the idol of moons
is off once more in undertones

the loop shepherds of bouncing
are all in thickets of leaving
the left paramours lichens too
o the wings and gun metal stew
coming to with winter ferocity
a dark so dramatised by beauty

parlance he did not beg a moon
become the watery option pools
that over scathing photocopies
saw a mechanical prefect knife
in to something and such peels
all grips to style with blanks

things they are no matter zone
to florid bunks done low drove
in malled algorithms and gloom
dusting the aggro of the spine
but too bad for green tills or
simple threats to a sure grout

THENCE THIS MUST

the rumbled sleeper tracks
the tardigrade tun to tune

mortified now cryptobiosis
machines for evening lungs

that mew to basic research
that nets down off screams

set smoother loose singing
stray near vague familiars

for squat stark statistics
for nostalgia read bad air

thumbs up the gothic whirl
mute throats so risk aware

under claustrophobic songs
the great orb in open noun

FULL-TIME CASSANDRAS

part subversive, part
hegemonic dud uh-huhs

aspirating folk combs
harp blood provenance

then post-orientalist
to much fracked water

espresso to dude waxy
white man for mammals

go slow the humanisms
self-puffer musculars

be home for the weeds
the zeal of the darks

hip for indo-european
inducing body swerves

to embrace in the pit
adults go speculating

see you in the arcade
the lichens are on me

OUTSPOKEN
for Omar Hazek

'In my songs the sea is azure'

even in Alexandaria the lichens do not speak
do not do televised azure folded to oblivion
but as some rift of dissident lung to rights
what rights, what spokes of broken mediation
what planet car gone harsh in sulphuric salt
                how our peripheral industry
                sews its productive horizon
                under cover of shy darkness
                lit for the invading reader
                and the edge all system tun
the legal recourse counts for zip gone windy
murmurations in the contrails blinding birds
the very flinch become a silver lining doing
as corruption gives, is, springs for markets
or contractual patter done into state wither
                    but white lies matter
                    white lies and public
                    shrouds the truth log
                    talking up into media
                    and so cut to purpose
          reason stands to argue the shunts
          soon enough, soon enough, severed
          into such broke whispers never to
          sign up for an open source duster
          with an extraction fan for oxygen
trade that and you trade the very conditions
there as some mirror of all in the burnt air
an evolutionary advantage inscribed in twigs
in judges and paid hands embracing cover ups
before turning to the philology of rope song

the candle flickers with mischief
the wax is not yet made of humans
nor of each still burning library
the carbon stanza and melt waters
that the corrupt so scarcely know
                    up close and lichen
                    mispronounced bokeh
                    on in darkest maths
                    the so so death gag
                    is in good standing
the city of Cafavy can still stir
for something other than the news
of noun cloning in the press pack
stung to pith by fresh allegation
mounting evidence of a complicity
as the cities spread their plastic toys over
the beach of broken tombeaux, shelf on shelf
where the grammarians encounter their makers
where the fleeing peoples bear the bodies of
children on their backs and press on to live
                    the aperture and blur flares
                    do shallow depths and fields
                    compromising in every detail
                    with the sour ideals dancing
                    over pea soups and tail coma
let the records show how the productivity of
lichens does air strains by so many per cent
the sulphur dioxide in the very art of mines
making good to fix the nitrogen of publicity
and then some, some coal tracer burning star

SPECIES COMPANIONS ARE US

to rust and livery sprawl
the velvet surrealists as
comrades still after this

to be so the heady helium
up up in the dilapidation
is that the noun schooner

with a look in their eyes
going go on be my species
people are a weeping wall

vividly in binding trance
down to the data scramble
where the berries do fire

it is this surely verdant
dross with the grump bled
we just need a bigger hut

the moth architecture for
reprising dark mutations:
smile to become exemplary

THE BALLAD OF LIBERAL MOONSHINE

how come is in patient darkness
as the cycles of representation
lay louder, darker on acid free
oracles to scarcer leatherbacks

bones so drawn to reading rooms
that sound flippers go autumnal
down still rarer critical forms
endangering the spineless light

scan yellowed meat sky forevers
into some imperilled species of
our loves and sun marked up for
preservations as reserve counts

that once defective music wants
to be for keeps not some anthem
to yet more but mutual research
collaring the flaming notebooks

for what then save the leathers
come waltzing in on historicism
such impostors frankly draining
what might pass off in property

over chromatic chorus polluters
also known as evolution's froth
with fresh sorry thanks for the
cinder toned dark ridge or keel

our every book upon book making
shallow depressions for lasting
dregs blistered all round again
down smiles for the old quarter

an off duty stamp in break neck
Vermeers for the window on work
on some long evensong among the
clearings come deforested songs

pages torn from the big dust up
that by its nature wants to see
action not bland literary tones
doing the spread scree darkness

murdering song with fire! fire!
how we laugh for peace brigades
and see dour scared rabbit ears
souring yet more sounding irony

this trade tap in coffee chains
says nature is just dead carbon
without the seconders proposing
the stakeholder presumed guilty

associated capitals do a stench
of dump trucks & wildfire skips
how lax this defining of pathos
has become all bar one survival

third nature over nature amidst
death by water spreading hearty
pesticides the margin bellowing
sulphur going yeah in the drink

for the decline of the incloser
aging amid every new reserve in
sum of the day our daily crater
with moonshine clear and glossy

as the flâneur strolled arcadia
a turtle on his leash, who knew
how flowers of capital inscribe
natural history in solar colour

a night turns a something green
come pleasure open for business
who knew the bloody whale songs
clogging seas like marine snow

INVENTORY SYNTHESIS

such moisture available
as to spread the thread
tips hardly stills such
orange explosions or in
harmony of wind-scoured
habitats goes to show a
spirit song of grammars
how to grieve in syntax

in to include colophons
the literature cited as
contents to index spars
spurs to injure a bench
or jury tuning abstract
turns then acknowledged
in with data as bedrock
or substrate as variety

the analyses are now in
and the results bespeak
pairwise comparisons of
splendour as befits the
plunder of spirit shown
forth to the merest due
among page macrolichens
hanging on shorn serifs

on some ordination axis
of human artifice sites
laid out in a dominated
grading show elevations
from the limited middle
the broken scope of law
driven into even wilder
natures assumed to fail

as a nature in question
there is none but spent
chemical signals at one
end and chemistry loves
exposed to a vegetation
so overwhelmed by scale
that the arctic is home
to what transcends this

moreover this trend was
associated with sublime
moss the broke moulding
into shower curtains as
some of the most remote
public land is trending
yes that's the sampling
biomass spread out thin

even so birds and small
mammals use lichens for
nesting matter to dwell
among the nutrient-poor
log of an anthropogenic
climate as oh now marks
the spot where occasion
has become system death

we are still but chosen
by our noise solidarity
that remains some floor
if not the land covered
data plots wished on in
defiance of buffer line
or aligned points lying
in for transect screens

each point out screened
to avoid isolated pixel
growth is only protocol
savvy for data collects
and spirit is in hunger
still in the inadequate
in helicopter plot logs
and pack dunes tendered

along in random azimuth
plot edges were flagged
up or in train to pages
shown the typical place
where landmarks are the
tokens of core strength
periods and commas held
up as its broken middle

on reflection the cited
characteristics fade to
bare incident radiation
duff or obvious litters
where the letters of us
cannot quite grip tears
a fleeting weather grid
embraced as the archive

in electronic copies of
raw community are shown
the slip the field note
as said to follow later
in the future synthesis
worth waiting up for if
the evidence is trusted
rather than simply lost

alpha and gamma sampler
graves are marked up as
emblems of forgotten or
nonparametric processes
as the jacknife methods
dress up in finer notes
of caution how to shade
and do in skewed totals

outliers found new land
cover strata identified
as sparse in no habitat
to speak of but average
richness values killing
in main point clouds or
class cover scales that
mix up the petrol count

transformation needs in
the environmental value
go beyond many multiple
random starting figures
as real data iterations
are ever preferred over
the otherwise desirable
the old song of the raw

what raw to grasp cover
sheets and skewness due
the best fitting stress
design and in full view
of a prevailing organic
view that is at best an
acid-loving song and no
argument worth its rain

PREVAILING WITH THE BEAUTIFUL
for Dell

if then, well the thing is
here's my cut cloth, would
you offset the bias & more
after the darker ages draw
lichen on, but run with on
flaming cloud marked up as
for northern lights, azure
failing and yes in detail

scarcely a pirate in sight
hails sweet privatisations
whose companion species is
said drone so brimming and
with big dog fur, ovations
and bright painted penguin
in the mix, how you and me
lose at identity politics

got the middles again, but
not a pillow kick starting
whole scales of nomination

and such orchestra failure
of you, me and the oranges
if the sun didn't worth it
that's climate change then
and folks for the species

the hook is, wouldn't know
how to dress up some dodgy
dossier for the verse ruse
exit sign, I grant you the
darker demeanour, the smog
quaintly called a prospect
and the hunkered down view
of a nuclear unit sans us

you count yourself a lucky
unit in accounts but spell
nought to still the greens
to the piano of lichens or
come dreams of some lie-in
and swatches, spent lemons
on the bar, the olives yet
to be shown their martini

loser to the enthusiasm do
to the scandal, it's gloss
be brave, more blue strewn
to some fishing quota, the
diving in gravity with the
anthropocene indeterminacy
moving over us like floods
of mom and dad, bass lite

friend, comma, mixing desk
lend me your soft software
that the wall is in dark a

decent Jericho, not summer
grass in homeland security
before post-baronial crass
is another name for middle
class news following wars

well of course you get it,
who doesn't, announcements
of the daily fire woven in
summer and breath of death
some great democratic yeah
with daft soap to minimize
the collateral damage, the
mark up over an extinction
how this species burns us

from one amoeba to another
and which in sickness talk
also known as an attack of
killer exclamations, marks
that smash it, marks grown
the stronger until even so
how each cell wall becomes
still yours and shimmering

REINDEER LICHEN

some for trophies some to flag
in canvas imperial some to lie
blinded by prospects of relics
scarce quick to a lichen trail
subsisting through the poo-jok
welcome to anthropogenic gases

our polluting breath one cloud
after another sung oft & aloft
tracers to cap data in cuilkuq
and beyond this arctic haze by
any other misnomer would smell
as rank in source signature of
Eurasian air the name spelling
car lungs into the troposphere
and albedo as the polar scalps
warm to softly falling sulphur
& carbons settling on cladonia
rangiferina misnamed cryptogam
or reindeer moss but still led
through by radionuclides taken
in along so-called food chains
what price pristine now & ever
wilds spent to a chemical sink
the sheet like flows so turbid
so given over to written scree

CRYPSIS PAPERS

industrial melanism eats in dark font
the stain and copper bottom dot irony

page based as to pale recessive moths
all mirror gone stalls to little cars

for one they like to spell gene death
care of the cropped man from Monsanto

toy punk in the locks of a cocked hat
depositing eggs on a cryptic bracelet

in what can only be called extinction
by a thousand shifts of dazzled heart

coming round to predation of all form
all incline frequencies faking salads

the lichen's mite does widow in looms
such cash & carry bliss for the foyer

and an unbreakable convention of care
in the write up of the glossy scruple

PARTICULATES

no, they'll want you down and dirty
every last log in the owned natural
and with wildly tortured affections
in organic spelling on and on until
they have you in their sugared palm
and can spell the plastic victories
            blooming energies gone liner nothings
            remains unread down a purple symmetry
            how quantum skips over mr white space
            without font matter in bliss of wimps
            quirk all told in the colliding gloom
                        clamping life
                        to the thread
                        cars in a nod
in contrails of every soft beverage
every subliminal advert saying burn
with you, yes you, nailed to chokes
and buttered parsnips of image fire
            tune over easy in the chemical

humanities where the molecular
LEDs and dongles show sackbuts
the caged canaries in agronomy
　　　　　or in clones, found paths
　　　　　to dawn in scanning prose
　　　　　this too a spent gleaning
　　　　　and all bookish asterisks
　　　　　in courts of fossil plant
　　　　　　　　dream not of pens
　　　　　　　　that are syringes
　　　　　　　　of darker ecology
　　　　　such succour made to ease
　　　　　as to surf up onto frozen
　　　　　drifts giving up to nouns
　　　　　　　　dream only clouds
　　　　　　　　in lichen archive
　　　　　　　　in before any law
　　　　　oh pass the harmonium the
　　　　　sick bucket oh and parcel
　　　　　postage stamps as lichens
　　　　　　　　to dazzling torts
　　　　　　　　amid group haunts
　　　　　　　　and fleet returns
　　　　　cushions to harbour sleet
　　　　　where the word limit hugs
　　　　　itself to a brevity thing
　　　　　finding in darks the keep
　　　　　giving up the art realtor
tuning up diamonds as lichen stars
standing room only for nightingales
beside the nitrogen fixing subtexts
　　　　　　the swift bubble wrapping
　　　　　　to compose a fresh miasma
　　　　　　　　dream on, toggled
　　　　　　　　scum for scumbles
　　　　　　　　dead to abstracts

and the stew in the bland
aporia of our ancient dog
come music hall analogies
all flagging guns
all spin to drift
the market strain
not quite the ticket moss
or lichens of sun sliding
to make a vengeance plaza
but then the slow
over canvas slips
in the real stain
some hunt of the cloud
getting set for stones
over air-born or spall
postage stamps on light carbon
the water marks carping and as
concrete ode on brutalist soil
all done the going slumps
by the name of not unless
there a talk as of recall
and toss records, grand revelations
to make up percentages as something
resembling nothing so much as verbs

SYMBOLISTE PROPAGANDA

splendid grime grooms every niche
then capers mene mene on the wall
the fairest of them all gone wild
each pending extinction wins gold
such smog tripe of the liberals
will not save us from affective

soteriology and pop drones come
lichens said in darkest capital
decking out a rhapsodic wilding
dark symbolistes of revolutions
that are not televised for this
this lichen is in on the detail
well a manuscript without lichens is
a score without grace notes how each
air balloon's at sea on songs in sun

        to the skip of dreams
        which felt stops sing
        come break the moulds
        and the oompah oompah

so lichens are a sloth's best friend
to be in sympathy with the symbiotic
front load stool of oblivion spawned
out of acronyms set in bone such are
the lichens of capital the efficient
flock wallpaper of disaster flicks o

        rocks without lichens are books
        without leaves not even a ghost
        to give up and give the lie the
        crushing finite bruised skyline
        how lichens are typographers of
        oxgen sewing serifs into azures
        then lichens for postage stamps
        of dark ecology and revolutions
        with water marks in done smiles
        this head to lay down down here

                here on the hinge of
                third nature there's
                no thing so critical
                as outlaws taking up
                the epic undo and so
                to the sweet refrain

a garden without lichens
is a garden without hope
as variation sprouts rote
there goes the proxy shit
giving the grammar ladder
made substrate and trends
for the breather workshop
what price lichen envy
in the landskip squall
mot in ideas but cloud
stalls for physic eyes
x marks the complex crux of spelt litters
how a lichen is a sign containing natures
coming to in stigmata amid printed matter
how postage stamps are become the lichens
of industrial revolution and of nostalgia
and of found mosaics in classical montage
as the digital type forms the known scars
as it will become some party
or even a leftist light sect
of the best before just poor
to slur in the better tenses
on dappled fonts as a stuffy
picturesque grammar and this
this patter drum does theory
a lichen is a poem containing theory
containing archives containing every
thing that the good boy deserves for
favour sucks until his digital thumb
becomes an ideogram on a digital bow
oh doesn't orange rhyme with lozenge
and as no such thing as free lichens
but still or mightier than the sward
not to mention have nots yes in eyes
every dark monument in lichen lining

it won't wash and don't count
the unsung work is never done
as barks in soundbites so sew
the sung to pixelated lichens
           roughly speaking
           barbs even wires
           over the scumble

INDEX OF TITLES

Titles of publications and sequences, including those that double up as titles of individual poems, are provided in italics.